That's Funny, You Don't Look Buddhist

Also by Sylvia Boorstein

It's Easier Than You Think:
The Buddhist Way to Happiness

Don't Just Do Something, Sit There:
A Mindfulness Retreat

That's Funny, You Don't Look Buddhist

ON BEING A FAITHFUL JEW
AND A PASSIONATE BUDDHIST

Sylvia Boorstein

FOREWORD BY STEPHEN MITCHELL

HarperSanFrancisco

An Imprint of HarperCollins*Publishers*

HarperSanFrancisco and the author, in association with The Basic
Foundation, a not-for-profit organization whose primary mission is refor-
estation, will facilitate the planting of two trees for every one tree used in the
manufacture of this book.

A TREE CLAUSE BOOK

HarperCollins Web Site: http://www.harpercollins.com
HarperCollins®, ☀®, HarperSanFrancisco™, and A TREE CLAUSE BOOK®
are trademarks of HarperCollins Publishers Inc.

FIRST EDITION

Library of Congress Cataloging-in-Publication Data
Boorstein, Sylvia.
That's funny, you don't look Buddhist: on being a faithful Jew and a pas-
sionate Buddhist / Sylvia Boorstein
ISBN 0–06–060957–5 (cloth)
ISBN 0–06–060958–3 (pbk.)
1. Buddhism–Relations–Judaism.   2. Judiasm–Relations–Buddhism.
1. Title.
BQ4610.J8B66   1996
296.3'872–dc20   96-16447

97 98 99 00 ❖ RRDH 10 9 8 7 6 5 4 3 2 1

For my grandmother
Leah Kanner Schor
1882–1949
who sang to me and told me stories.

Contents

Preface

I AM DEEPLY GRATEFUL to Sharon Lebell for her idea to write this book. It was her conception and her title that initiated this project. She was convinced that a book describing and interpreting the remarkably obvious strong presence of Jews in the growing Western Buddhist community would be timely. She did a wonderful book proposal and drafted the initial version of the book in fulfillment of that outline. Sharon's enthusiasm has been a sustaining factor throughout the book's unexpected evolution.

Our initial plan was that we would write, as coauthors, an overview of the "Jewish-Buddhist phenomenon": its demographics, the particular allure of Buddhism, the obvious congruences of the two traditions. We share the view that this contemporary looking beyond parochial boundaries reflects the broadminded spiritual interest that has been the hallmark of Judaism whenever it has not been under siege and is an important element in its remaining a living tradition. We thought that our two voices, as women a generation apart in age, with different backgrounds in Judaism as well as in Buddhism, would blend well as chroniclers because we bring different perspectives and are also good friends.

After a great deal of work independently, we discovered that our joint project as conceived was not viable. For me, the imperative of the book changed. People seemed less interested in "Why is this happening?" and more eager to know "How is it possible to be both a Jew and a Buddhist?" Their interest was personal, not general. They wanted to know, "How do *you* do it?" and "Can *I*?" That was not the book we planned to write, but it became the only book that I, in good conscience, could write.

Sharon has been most gracious in relinquishing her position in the book we had jointly envisioned. When we arrived at this new agreement, she said, "The biggest thing I've learned from writing this book is how to let go of attachments."

I feel that *That's Funny, You Don't Look Buddhist,* in its current form, remains true to our initial commitment to write the most honest and helpful book possible.

Foreword

BY STEPHEN MITCHELL

"Who is Sylvia? what is she?" It's not often that a writer gets to answer a question asked by Shakespeare. But my friend Sylvia Boorstein is lucky. She is in the right place at the right time, as are we all. She has, in addition to *who* and *what*, taken on the question of *how*: how she can be both an observant Jew and a passionately committed Buddhist. This book is her honest, funny, kind, charming answer. (Zen literature speaks of "grandmotherly kindness," the amused compassion of a bodhisattva, whose every act is for the benefit of all beings; it is the merest coincidence that Sylvia is a grandmother in the flesh.)

As we can see from these essays in self-awareness, you can be both a Jew and a Buddhist as comfortably as you can be both a Jew and a humanist. Ultimately, though, the issue of being either Jewish or Buddhist is irrelevant. "Don't be a Buddhist," one contemporary Buddhist teacher has advised: "be a Buddha." The deeper you go on any spiritual path, the less of a path there is. We talk of Judaism, Buddhism. But any -ism is a wasm, as Paul Krassner wittily observed. Beyond our thoughts of past and future, self and other, shines the infinitesimally vanishing, infinitely present truth, in which "Who am I?" has the same no-answer for each of us, because there is no question. The point of all spiritual practice is to wake up from the dream of a separate self. Once we realize who we are, it is possible to let the ancient, convoluted, jerry-built, unconscious mechanism of selfhood gratefully roll to a stop.

In Jewish terms, this is an issue of how, at the deepest level, we can fulfill the First Commandment, "You shall have no other gods before me." The only God worthy of our ultimate allegiance is the God whose true name is *Ehyéh*, "I Am" (a.k.a. *Ayin*, "Emptiness"). When we give our allegiance to something lesser, however holy it may be, we are worshiping an idol.

The first-century rabbi Hillel the Elder, in a famous story, had another way of stating the issue. When a pagan (how antiquated and narrowminded that term seems now; let's say, When a sincere and skeptical Roman citizen) asked him, "What is the essence of Judaism?," Hillel answered, "What you yourself hate, don't do to your neighbor. This is the whole Torah; the rest is commentary. Go now and learn it." Loving your neighbor as yourself—treating all beings, at all times, with respect and compassion—is equivalent to loving God with all your heart, the primal commandment. And loving God with all your heart is equivalent to understanding who you are. ("The more you understand yourself, the more you love God," our teacher Spinoza said.) But how do we "go and learn it"? Is it valid only if we go to a Jew? What if we learn it from a Hindu sage? from a Buddhist who has grown beyond the -ist? from a twinkly-eyed grandmotherly-kind Chinese pagan? God doesn't care where we learn it. God only cares *that* we learn it.

Even the greatest teachers, though, even the most profound traditions, can do nothing more than point the way to the truth. It is a figure of speech to say you can learn it *from* anyone. You can learn it only from yourself. And what, in the end, is there to learn? The Buddha himself said, "When I attained Absolute Perfect Enlightenment, I attained absolutely nothing." If it is worth attaining, it has already been attained. You step off the raft onto the glorious other shore, and all your friends and family are there, waving their handkerchiefs, wishing you bon voyage.

When we realize that nothing matters, we can appreciate that everything matters. The complementary truth about the irrelevance of being a Jew or a Buddhist is the vital importance of claiming or reclaiming our ancestry. "Who am I?—I am Sylvia Boorstein, *hineyni*: a Buddhist teacher, a Jewish learner." It is like coming to wholeness with our parents. We can't accept ourselves until we accept them, with all their flaws. And a further step: not only to accept them, but to honor them. This is called the Fifth Commandment.

For Sylvia, reclaiming the Jewish tradition is an act of piety. I find it deeply moving to know that this dear woman, having embodied what she has seen in her practice of the Dharma, goes to synagogue, lights the Sabbath candles, keeps a kosher home, and is herself deeply moved every time she can make a verse from the prayerbook or the Bible her own. One of her delighted jobs these days is teaching meditation to rabbis: showing them a simple, nonsectarian, powerful method of learning to understand themselves and love God with all their hearts. In the process of becoming genuine, she has become truly Jewish. And she looks more and more Buddhist as the years go by.

That's Funny, You Don't Look Buddhist

First Page

IN THE MIDDLE OF A BUDDHIST MEDITATION RETREAT, my mind filled with a peace I had not known before—completely restful, balanced, alert, joyous peace—and I said, "*Baruch Hashem*" (Praise God). The next thing I did was say the Hebrew blessing of thanksgiving for having lived long enough, for having been "sustained in life and allowed to reach" that day. The blessings arose spontaneously in my mind. I didn't plan them. My prayer life in those days was a memory rather than a habit, but the blessings felt entirely natural.

These days when students report experiences of their minds free of tension—clear and balanced and peaceful—I usually say something like: "This is great. This is an insight into the third Noble Truth of the Buddha. The end of suffering, an alert and contented mind, *is* possible, in this very lifetime, remembering *your* whole story, remembering *everyone's* whole story. The mind can hold it all—with equanimity, even with joy." I rejoice with them and for them.

I am grateful that I know two vocabularies of response. I think of one as my voice of understanding and the other as the voice of my heart.

One More River

I HAVE DISCOVERED THAT THE QUESTIONS MOST ASKED
of me by Jews are "how" questions. I am recognized as a
Buddhist. I am also—and have become much more open
about this part in the last few years—an observant Jew. Not
only more *open*, but also more observant. *Because* I am a
Buddhist. Because I have a meditation practice. So the
questions now are: "How did that happen?" "What is your
practice?" "Do you pray?" "To whom?" "Why?" "Do you
also do *metta* (lovingkindness) practice?" "When do you do
what?" "Why?" "What are your 'observances,' and why do
you do them?" "How do you deal with the patriarchal tone
of Jewish prayers?" "What is your relationship to the
Torah?" "To Buddhist scripture?" Most of all, "How can
you be a Buddhist and a Jew?" And, "Can I?"

The answer to the "how" questions requires that I tell
my personal story. Certainly not my story as a prescription
for anyone else, but to explain how my Buddhism has
made me more passionately alive as a Jew. And how my renewed Judaism has made me a better Buddhist teacher.

When I realized the degree of personal exposure that
telling my story would require, I became alarmed that I was
going to rock the boat. I had been quietly enjoying a private
life as a Jew and some new, pleasant recognition as a
Buddhist teacher. I had been accepting invitations for some
years to teach Jewish groups, and although I had worried
initially that they would be hostile about my Buddhism,
they weren't. They invited me back. Then I worried about
the Buddhists.

"What if the Buddhists get mad at me for not renouncing Judaism?"

Clearly, this was *my* issue, not anyone else's. No one is mad at me. I've been announcing myself, regularly, at Buddhist teachers' meetings, and it causes no ripple at all. I feel anticipatory alarm, I tell my truth, and it is completely a nonevent.

Recently I was one of twenty-six teachers meeting with the Dalai Lama in Dharamsala, India, to discuss how we are teaching Buddhism in the West. As part of the preparation for our meeting, we each answered the question, "What is the greatest current spiritual challenge in your practice and teaching?"

I thought, "Okay, this is it! These are major teachers in all lineages, these are people I respect and who I hope will respect me." And I said my truth: "I am a Jew. These days I spend a lot of my time teaching Buddhist meditation to Jews. It gives me special pleasure to teach Jews, and sometimes special problems. I feel it's my calling, though, something I'm supposed to do. And I'm worried that someone here will think I'm doing something wrong. Someone will say, 'You're not a *real* Buddhist!'"

It was another nonevent. I think—I hope—that was the "One Last River to Cross." I never did ask the Dalai Lama if what I am doing is okay. It had become, for me, a nonquestion by the time we got to our meetings with him. My particular group discussed "Lay and Monastic Practice in the West," and I did say, "I am a Jew, and monasticism is not part of Jewish tradition." I'm not entirely sure of the context in which I made that remark. It may not have been completely relevant to the discussion. Perhaps it was prompted by my desire to make *sure* I made my declaration publicly, in Dharamsala to the Dalai Lama, just in case that might emerge later as "one more river."

The three-hour return taxi ride from Dharamsala to Pathankot was occasionally hair-raising. Indian taxis are truly dangerous. Accidents, fatal ones, are common. I was sitting in front with the driver, trying to maintain some composure in the face of many last-minute reprieves. As we passed through one particular section of narrow mountain road, there were a few swerves that brought the taxi very close to the edge.

My friend Jack Kornfield was sitting with Steve Smith and Heinz Roiger in the backseat.

Jack said, "I hope you are saying protection mantras, Sylvia."

I said, "Of course I am."

He said, "Are they Jewish mantras or Buddhist mantras?"

I said, "Both."

Jack laughed. "Good."

I Am a Jew and I Am a Buddhist

I AM A JEW BECAUSE MY PARENTS WERE MILD-MANNERED, cheerful best friends who loved me enormously, and they were Jews. It's my karma. It's good karma. My parents' love included respect, admiration, high expectations, and a tremendous amount of permission. I can't remember ever being scolded.

I am a prayerful, devout Jew because I am a Buddhist. As the meditation practice that I learned from my Buddhist teachers made me less fearful and allowed me to fall in love with life, I discovered that the prayer language of "thank-you" that I knew from my childhood returned, spontaneously and to my great delight. From the very first day of my very first Buddhist meditation retreat, from the very first time I heard the Buddha's elegant and succinct teachings about the possibility of the end of suffering—not the end of pain, but the end of suffering—I was captivated, I was thrilled, and I was reassured. The idea that it was possible, in the middle of this very life, fully engaged in life, to live contentedly and compassionately was completely compelling. I felt better even before I *was* better.

It took me a long time, even after I had begun to teach Buddhist meditation, to get ready to say, "I am a Buddhist." I often hesitated. I circumlocuted. I said, when pressed to identify myself, "I am a Dharma teacher," or "I teach Buddhist psychology," or "I am a Buddhist meditation teacher." To say, "I am a Buddhist" seemed too much like taking a plunge that I didn't need to take.

Ten years ago I was a Buddhist delegate at an international interfaith women's conference in Toronto. There were two other Buddhist delegates, Chatsumaran Kabalsingh and Judith Simmer-Brown, both of whom had more impressive Buddhist vitae than I did. Eight Jewish women, some of them famous, were delegates as well. I was nervous about them, wondering if they were thinking, "What's a nice Jewish girl like you doing as a Buddhist delegate?"

On the first day of the conference all the delegates, sixty of us, stood up in turn around the large, rectangular table at which we were all seated and identified ourselves by name and religious affiliation. People were normally succinct. "My name is So-and-so. I am a Jew." "My name is So-and-so. I am a Catholic." I'm fairly sure that Judith and Chat introduced themselves as Buddhists. When I stood up, I said, "My name is Sylvia Boorstein. I grew up as a Jew, and I teach Buddhist meditation." Both statements were true, but neither of them was the whole story. I felt awkward about what I said, but it was the best I could do at the time.

One evening, as part of the program, all the delegates took a field trip to visit a mosque, a Buddhist temple, and a synagogue. In the Buddhist temple an Asian couple were doing prostrations by themselves in front of huge, gilt Buddha statues. The local abbot gave a far-too-parochial, far-too-sexist introduction to Buddhism than was appropriate for this group of sophisticated women. I glanced around, uneasy. "What are all these women thinking about Buddhism? What are the Jewish women thinking about *me*?"

In the synagogue the rabbi and the cantor (both men) gave an introduction to High Holy Day observance that would have convinced anyone (including Jews, I think) that liturgy is nonparticipatory. I was too busy feeling awkward about sitting in the back of the synagogue with Chat and Judith instead of with the Jews who sat up front to worry about the rabbi and the cantor. The Jews worried, though. I overheard them grumbling afterward.

In the social hall later on, while we were drinking tea, the president of the temple sisterhood cordially inquired, "And which group are you with?" I said, "I teach Buddhist meditation." Startled eyebrow reaction and sincerely surprised exclamation: "That's funny," she said, "you don't *look* Buddhist!"

That evening was, perhaps, the nadir of my spiritual identity. I remember feeling lonely and isolated on the bus ride home. I thought, "I am a person without a country. I'm not anything."

The following evening, the Wiccan women at the conference announced that they would conduct a Wiccan ritual and invited any delegate who was interested to join them. Margot Adler was one of the Wiccan delegates, and by that point in the week I had met Margot and we'd spent some time together enjoying making friends with each other and discovering the similarities in our backgrounds. My recollection is that we sat on the bed in one of our dormitory rooms and sang old camp songs together.

I decided to go to the Wiccan ceremony. Many, but not all, of the other conference delegates were there. I recall thinking that to Westerners, Wicca is even more suspicious than Buddhism. The first ritual of the evening was a formation of a circle. And the first instruction was "Now let's go around the circle one by one and each of us say our names and our religious identity." I was still reverberating, unhappily, from my identity crisis of the previous evening. "Oh,

God," I thought, "here we go again." Once again people went around the circle identifying themselves, "I am So-and-so and I'm a such-and-such." Just before my turn approached, I heard a voice—who knows who, my psyche, my *maggid*—a voice that said, "Go for it." I said, "My name is Sylvia. I am a Buddhist." Nothing happened. Lightning did not strike. The circle of identification continued. I felt good.

Near the end of our week together, Deborah, one of the Jewish delegates, a woman who lived in Jerusalem, invited me to have breakfast with her. She told me that the Jewish delegates really *had* been wondering about me and had, in fact, hesitated to speak to me directly. She felt ready to, she said, because she was, like myself, a New Yorker, the child of Eastern European immigrant Jews, and a Barnard alumna. We had the same education. She was living in an orthodox religious commune in Jerusalem, one that was working actively toward Israeli-Palestinian reconciliation. A passionate, *frum* (orthodox), socially engaged Jew. I admired her. I also didn't feel judged by her. I felt I had distinguished myself during the week with whatever remarks I had made, more as a psychologist than as a Buddhist scholar, and I felt that she admired me.

"I never stopped being a Jew," I told her, "and I have very affectionate feelings for Judaism. Ten years ago, though, I found myself frightened, alarmed about the fragility of life. Because it was the seventies and meditation and Eastern philosophy were becoming popular in the West, and I think, because of grace, I met some Buddhist teachers who spoke to the very issues I was frightened about. Before I met them, I didn't even know that it was spiritual understanding and spiritual solace that I was lacking. Maybe if I had known, I would have sought out a

Jewish spiritual teacher." I saw that Deborah was listening carefully to what I said, and I continued on, perhaps hurriedly anticipating her telling me that there were Jewish spiritual teachers as well.

"Since that time," I told her, "I've read Herbert Weiner's 9 1/2 *Mystics* and I now know that there are Jewish teachers as well. Maybe if I had met one of them, I would have had an entirely different path."

Deborah hesitated for just a moment before she spoke. "Maybe," she said, "maybe you would have had a different path if one of them had been willing to teach women."

I felt dismayed. I had meant to protect myself and inadvertently, I thought, made her vulnerable. Now, as I recall the moment, I think it's unlikely that Deborah felt vulnerable. She was the kind of woman who could be both orthodox and broad-minded, religiously parochial and spiritually universal. If anything was exposed as vulnerable in that moment it was Judaism, vulnerable to the criticism that its most profound teachings were not universally accessible and certainly not universally accessible to women.

Deborah and I smiled at each other. "I'm glad we spoke," she said.

"So am I," I answered.

Chat Kabalsingh later told me that some of the Asian delegates had asked her about Judith Simmer-Brown and me, suggesting that as non-Asians we couldn't be real Buddhists. I am a real Buddhist. I'm not an ethnic Buddhist, but I'm a real Buddhist, and I'm also a Jew. I'm not a person without a country. I am a person who has dual citizenship.

My childhood as a Jewish girl growing up in Brooklyn in the 1940s was overwhelmingly a pleasant one. My parents' family circle was close-knit and, culturally and comfortably, completely Jewish. When I was teased at school—I was the only Jew in my class and anti-Semitism was high in those days—my parents arranged for me to transfer to the neighboring, primarily Jewish, school district. I spent afternoons in a Yiddish Folkshule happily avoiding what seemed to me the dreary Talmud Torah (religious school) associated with our synagogue. I spent summers at Kinderwelt, a children's camp run by the Jewish National Workers' Alliance, an organization that was, apparently paradoxically, ritually orthodox, passionately Zionist, and intellectually modern. I was an only child, and my father, in a culture known to have preferred boys, thought I was wonderful.

My pleasant childhood experiences have everything to do with why I am a Jew and nothing at all to do with why I am a Buddhist. Some of the early Jewish-Buddhist dialogue linked—erroneously, I believe—"bad experiences of a Jewish childhood" stories to "this is what attracted me, as an adult, to Buddhism" stories. Linking one set of stories with the other creates extra confusion. It's like drawing *random* lines in a Connect-the-Dots book. No clear image emerges. Probably the idea that unfortunate Jewish experiences *created* an interest in Buddhism and that the interest in Buddhism therefore reflects poorly on Judaism is what has added to Jewish concern and to the intensity of the dialogue.

Rabbi Jonathan Omer-Man, Rabbi Miles Krassen, and I led a discussion group about the interest of Jews in Buddhism at Elat Chayyim, a Jewish Renewal Center, in the summer of 1993. The room was full—more than a hundred people.

"But *why* are Jews so interested in Buddhism?"

Miles went first. Miles is professor of Judaic studies at Oberlin College, and he spoke, out of his own experience, of what he found had been underemphasized, hard to find in Judaism: meditation, solitude, introspection, contemplative space.

"But why are *Jews* so interested in Buddhism?"

I went next. I talked about how Judaism's high regard for scholarship, for inquiry and—at least in America in this century—its genuine, ecumenical respect had encouraged and allowed passionate young Jews dedicated to spiritual search to look at other spiritual traditions.

"But why are Jews so interested in *Buddhism?*"

Jonathan was, in his inimitable way, succinct: "Jews are interested in Buddhism because it is a complete, mature, sophisticated spiritual path."

Miles's answer was certainly helpful. It *does* provide a clue, structurally, to a dimension of spiritual experience that has been missing for Jews. It hints at the truth that the mind has—as its essence—the clarity from which wisdom arises. It also implies that a full religious path must include tools for accessing that essence directly.

My answer—Jewish ecumenism and Jewish intellectual focus—was mostly irrelevant. Probably it came from my habit of trying to make people (in this case, Jews) feel good about themselves as well as from my position of being a Buddhist between two substantially credentialled Jews. Mine was a *sweet* answer—partly true, but certainly open to debate. Not all Jews are intellectual, and certainly not everyone's family or congregation has open-minded views. Even if it were true, it doesn't answer the questions, "What were they looking for?" and "Why Buddhism?"

Jonathan's answer, dramatic enough to almost end the conversation, was closest to the truth. The Buddhism that had come to the West offered a clear explanation for suffering and tools for the direct, personal realization of a peaceful mind. It required practice, not affiliation. It was a great spiritual *path*. It promised transformation.

An Early Introduction to Buddhism

I WAS BORN IN NEW YORK CITY IN 1936. MY PARENTS, Harry and Gladys Schor, met as neighbors in Coney Island, at that time an enclave of Eastern European immigrant Jews at the beach end of Brooklyn. I was an only child and an only grandchild. I lived with my parents and my father's parents in an apartment around the corner from my mother's family. My grandfather died soon after I was born and both my parents worked at full-time jobs, so my grandmother was my principal caregiver. I am fairly sure that my first language was Yiddish.

I think of my grandmother as my first Buddhist teacher. She was completely sensible. My grandfather had left her in Poland when my father was a year old, promising to send for them as soon as he earned money for their passage. World War I broke out soon after, and my grandmother spent eight years alone with my father, several of them in refugee camps, before she could emigrate.

My grandfather never earned very much—he sewed the front sides of boys' pants in a piecework garment factory—and my grandmother took in boarders to augment their income. I never heard these stories as complaints. I heard them as reminiscences, stories my mother told about my grandmother's capacity to take care of people. My mother said she had agreed to marry my father only if he promised to ask his mother to stop buttering his bread.

My grandmother was entirely solicitous of all my physical needs. She cooked things I liked. We took walks together. She bathed and dressed me and braided my hair.

She sat by my bedside and sang to me until I fell asleep. And she was sensibly philosophical about my moods. Sadness didn't worry her. On those occasions—which must have been frequent enough for me to remember—when I said, "But I'm not happy!" she would say, "Where is it written that you are supposed to be happy all the time?" She must have said it kindly, because I don't remember it as a rebuke, and I think of it now as my introduction to the first of the Four Noble Truths of the Buddha. Life is difficult. Just because it is. Because things change. Because change means loss and disappointment. Because bodies and relationships are, from time to time, painful. I was reassured by my grandmother's response. I didn't feel I was making a mistake by feeling sad, and she didn't feel obliged to fix me.

Good Karma

From a childhood of Sabbaths spent in the East Third Street Shul (synagogue), two regular, repetitive events seem to me cornerstones of my religious consciousness. I credit one with being the foundation of my sense of being okay, just as I am. The other I imagine as my first impression of what is meant by a personal relationship with God. Neither event was liturgical, but they couldn't have happened anywhere else.

The East Third Street Shul was actually one large room several steps down from street level. The front doors opened onto the steps that led to a small entrance foyer flanked on one side by toilets, on the other by a small room for standing-up, schnapps and herring and honey-cake *kiddushes* (receptions that include blessings) after services. The main room had a wide middle section for men, one side aisle section for men, and seats up front on the *bimah* (raised altar space) for important men. The women sat in the aisle section on the other side, apart from the men. Everyone sat on folding chairs.

My grandmother and I walked to *shul* together every Saturday and always arrived early. She stayed in her usual place, two seats in from the side wall, throughout the morning. I divided my time. I would sit for a while next to my grandmother, looking around and listening. I remember enjoying how the swaying, singing men, who all seemed to be out of sync with each other, would, from time to time, appear to catch up. When I got bored with listening, I'd go outdoors into the courtyard and play Ring-O-Leevio or flip baseball trading cards with my friends.

Each return to my seat next to my grandmother required that I squeeze by the legs of six or seven old women who shared her row. I recall that view as one of knees, elastic stockings, and canes. The women would look at me over their prayer books and grumble in Yiddish: "The child is creeping in and out too much."

My grandmother was completely unruffled by their complaints, unstinting in her support. "Leave her alone," she would say. "She is fine."

Mrs. Levy, my friend Eleanor's grandmother, sat in the row in front of us. On one of my trips in or out, Mrs. Levy would sense my presence behind her and swivel her head around to talk to me. Peering over her wire glasses, she would whisper: "'Ow's mudder?"

Mrs. Levy's daughter and my mother both had rheumatic heart disease, and Mrs. Levy worried for both of them.

"She's fine, Mrs. Levy," I would whisper back.

Mrs. Levy would look back down into her prayer book. "Tenks, God," she would say.

I was always touched by Mrs. Levy's response, which seemed to me special. People regularly asked about my mother's health. Most often the response to my positive reassurance was "Thank God for that!" It always sounded like an instruction to me, a reminder that I should thank God. Mrs. Levy's response was not directed at me. It was her response to God. "Thanks."

"So, What's a Nice Jewish Girl Like You . . . ?"

WHEN I WAS GROWING UP, MY FATHER USED TO SAY, probably in an attempt to cheer up dismal situations, "Everything is for the best in this the best of all possible worlds." He was citing Voltaire, and *Candide* is satire, but I didn't know that. I thought my father was just being mysterious, because "everything is for the best" was not my experience. I would have preferred that my mother were healthy—her heart ailment worried me throughout my childhood—and I knew that my father would have, too. Panglossian philosophy isn't good Buddhist thinking, either. It's making up a story, elaborating a plain fact. Everything is just what it is. "For the best" is a story, an interpretation that presumes motive.

I also make up stories elaborating facts, inferring cause. One of my favorite stories is: "God and my grandmother arranged for me to meet Seymour, who as part of his zealous spiritual search, would introduce *me* to Buddhism, thereby beginning a chain of events that culminates in my teaching Dharma and meditation." I can string the facts of my life together—not *all* the facts, just some particular facts—so that, if my listeners are as romantic as I am, they might enjoy the story as much as I do. I'd have to tell my story quickly, though, and then run off and hide before my Buddhist friends caught up with me shouting, "Delusion! Delusion!"

They would be right, of course. Things are just what they are. Everything is *related* to everything else—(really to *everything* else, so choosing specific details to make a story makes *a* story, not *the* story)—and inferring intentional motives is extra.

Caveat Emptor: Here's the story anyway. I met Seymour when I was fifteen years old, pretending to be eighteen so I could have a job. We met at a Jewish children's camp, were married three years later, and one year after our marriage—after we'd both finished school—we moved to Topeka, Kansas, where he began a psychiatric residency at The Menninger Clinic. We both taught Sunday School, and Michael and Elizabeth, the first two of our four children, were born. The sweetest Jewish story of the three Topeka years was probably the secret collection the Jewish community took up on our behalf to pay for a *mohel* to come from Kansas City for Michael's *bris* (circumcision). One of the saddest Jewish stories was my in-laws' refusal to come to Topeka for Michael's *bris* because we were no longer *kashrut* (dietary) observant. A third Jewish story, one that I've told sometimes as a pivotal point in my religious history, is the account of the man standing next to me at Yom Kippur services doing a running *sotto voce* mocking commentary during the Recitation of Sins. The list of transgressions is serious; his additions trivialized them. I thought he sounded witty and sophisticated, and so I felt naive and embarrassed. Probably the Yom Kippur story *was* pivotal in how my story unfolded, because I remember it. Ultimately, though, it's not the stories that determine our choices, but the stories we continue to choose.

Ten years, two more children (Peter and Emily), and a master's degree in social welfare later, I was working as a psychotherapist in California, actively engaged in peace and civil rights causes and minimally engaged with Judaism. No dramatic parting of the ways had ever happened. In fact, good stories had happened. When I presented myself, with my twelve-year-old eldest child, to the rabbi of the Reform Synagogue and said, "This is Michael. He's learned to read Hebrew by taking an adult education class in the local high school, and he'd like to have a bar mitzvah," the rabbi said, "I'll try to do it. I'll ask my board of directors." A week later he phoned and said, "The board says 'okay.' You can join the congregation if you decide to, but it's not necessary." We joined. We actually stayed joined for several years, through Peter's bar mitzvah, but membership was tangential to our lives. The congregation was socially active and politically progressive, but so was I, I felt, without it. And by that time, I was depressed and anxious about what I began to realize were going to be dilemmas in my life—loss and grief, inevitable pain—regardless of how peaceful or just the world became. I didn't know the phrase "existential angst"—pain just because of life itself—but even if I had and had recognized it in myself, I wouldn't have known its remedy. I had no idea that religion addressed that very question. My experience of religion had been that of club membership—an extended family circle in which members supported each other in times of difficulty. I also had no idea that religion offered answers—or better yet, provided clues and technical instructions and guidance so that club members could discover the answers for themselves.

Seymour figured out before I did that spiritual paths *should* have the answers. We joked about him being the Advance Spiritual Scout. He would try something new— Mind Dynamics, Transcendental Meditation, Actualism— and usually come home and say, "Syl, this is *it.*" After his first encounter with Buddhism—a mindfulness retreat—he encouraged me to go also. As usual, he said, "Syl, this is *it.*"

The first time I heard my Buddhist teachers explain the Four Noble Truths—beginning with "Life is *dukkha*" (unsatisfying, painful by its very nature, unreliable even when it is pleasant because it is always changing)—I thought, "They're telling the truth. These people are talking about exactly what I'm worried about. They know what the *real* problem is. And they promise a solution." My friend Howie Cohen, another Jew teaching Buddhism, told me, "The first time I heard the Four Noble Truths, I cried."

Basic Dharma

I WAS INTRODUCED TO BUDDHISM AT A TIME IN MY LIFE when I was frightened by my sense that life was too hard, too fragile, to accept without despair. I doubted it could be otherwise. I attended my first *Vipassana* (mindfulness) retreat in 1977. I think what most excited me (and many other Westerners) about Buddhism was that it offers a succinct explanation for suffering. It recognizes that pain is a given in life, but still offers the possibility of the end of suffering (by ending the extra pain of struggling with situations beyond our control).

The end of suffering, I learned, was something *I* could bring about through my own practice. It depended on me. And, I didn't have to *believe* it was true, or say I believed it was true, or make any declaration of faith at all. In fact, one of the first teachings I heard was the Buddha's sermon to the people of Kalama in which he said, in essence, "Don't believe anything anyone tells you—even if they are a friend or a teacher or even if they are the Buddha—do the practice yourself and see if it's true." A practice that I was invited to investigate without believing it was true was very appealing.

The first of the Four Noble Truths, the central teaching of the Buddha, is that life is fundamentally unsatisfying because of its fragility, its temporality. Nothing lasts. I was relieved to hear this as the starting point for practice. I had, by the time I discovered Buddhism, spent several years preoccupied with the notion that I was the only person I knew who recognized that life was tragically flawed, and yet here it was as the central teaching of the Buddha. It was such a relief! My reading of how life is was not a personal melancholy misperception. My *response* to it was melancholy, but here were teachers who said that it was possible to cultivate wiser responses. They were contemporaries of mine with backgrounds similar to mine, and they seemed happy.

The second of the Noble Truths differentiates between the inevitable pains of life and the extra pain created in the mind that struggles rather than accommodates. The words *attachment* and *clinging* are used to describe the tension that arises in the mind when it is unable to accept what is true. When I recognized the tension in my mind, I longed for the ability to let go of clinging and discovered how hard it was. I didn't feel *I* was clinging. I felt my attachments were clinging to *me*. Caught in the grip of a worry attack, or agonized when something was not well with one of my children, I resigned myself to passing through a particularly intense period in what seemed, at best, a life lived stepping gingerly between minefields of catastrophe. My heart was tense and guarded.

The third of the Noble Truths of the Buddha is the promise that peace of mind and a contented heart are not dependent upon external circumstances. I think it was this promise, so clearly articulated, that initially attracted Westerners. The fourth Noble Truth, the Eightfold Path of Practice, followed the promise of peace with straightforward instructions that were ordinary and accessible and made practice the context of life. Although for most of us Buddhism did not require a lifestyle change, we were committed to transformation. We counted on being changed by practice.

The Buddha was a monastic, but the practice of mindfulness in the context of *any* lifestyle is one of renunciation. Every moment of mindfulness renounces the reflexive, self-protecting response of the mind in favor of clear and balanced understanding. In the light of the wisdom that comes from balanced understanding, attachment to having things be other than what they are falls away.

A concern of some new meditators is that a peaceful heart doesn't allow for taking a stand, or acting decisively against injustice. This is particularly true for Jews, for whom the prophetic vision of social justice is a cornerstone of religious practice. My father, for instance, thought that a peaceful heart precluded forceful action. He used to say, "I *need* my anger. It obliges me to take action."

I think my father was partly right. Anger arises, naturally, to *signal* disturbing situations that might require action. But actions initiated in anger perpetuate suffering. The most effective actions are those conceived in the wisdom of clarity.

The Dalai Lama, responding to a question about what he thought he would be doing when he was old, said, "Maybe I'll live in a monastery in China. They have some lovely old Buddhist monasteries there." This seems, at first hearing, amazing. The Chinese have invaded Tibet, tortured and killed millions of Tibetans, and seem intent on erasing Tibetan culture and religion. On the other hand, boycotting the monasteries will not restore Tibet, so the Dalai Lama's response is sensible.

His response is more than sensible. It reflects his understanding that events unfold as a reflection of precise karmic order and that a benevolent response in all circumstances

will be the most healing one. I think he is so universally admired because he exemplifies by his behavior the truth that
the essence of natural mind, unclouded by greed or anger
or delusion, is that of peace.

All Attachments Cause Suffering

IN THE COURSE OF WRITING THIS BOOK, I'VE SUFFERED from the very attachment that I hoped this book would dispel. One motivation for writing was my hope that I could replace emphasis on religious *identity* with the idea of the importance of religious *aspiration*. I hoped that by telling my story and the stories of some of my friends, the questions "Am I a good Jew?", "Am I compromising myself as a Jew?", and "Have I become a Buddhist and what does that mean?" would change to "How am I progressing toward my goal of becoming a fully loving and compassionate person?" I thought I was no longer limited by attachment to parochial viewpoints. I discovered I was wrong.

When I told one of my Buddhist friends I was writing this book, he said to me, "Good, this means you're going to shine the light of the Dharma through Judaism." I thought to myself, "Wait a minute. That's not so nice to say about Judaism. That implies that Judaism doesn't have enough light to reveal the truth." Even though it had been true for me that Judaism had provided neither the answer nor the practice techniques I needed to discover the answer myself, my instinctive allegiance to Judaism caused my back to stiffen in opposition.

I didn't contest my friend's remark, perhaps because I knew I didn't have a good rebuttal. Probably I also let the remark pass by because my persona, to which I am also attached, is built around congeniality. I knew, even in the moment of internally leaping to the defense of Judaism, that my friend's remark had been couched in genuine respect and affection—both for me *and* for Judaism. My defensive stance, even unvoiced, was painful. I was suffering.

I also suffered in needless defense of Buddhism. Sometime in the past year a friend of mine recounted a conversation she had overheard in which people were discussing me. (Of course the fact that she was reporting the conversation, essentially transmitting gossip, was itself an example of the pain that arises from other than Right Speech—but that's another story.) What she reported was, "So-and-so said, 'Sylvia is really doing a great job these days teaching mindfulness to Jews. It's wonderful that she seems prepared to identify herself so publicly as a Jew. I wonder why she doesn't just drop that Buddhism business.'" I found myself becoming angry. I was feeling protective of myself and of Buddhism. "I don't give up the Buddhism," I thought, "because it's the way in which I understand life. It's crucial to me. Why on earth would I want to give it up?" I also thought, "*And* I wish people weren't talking about me." Probably if I had heard only flattering comments and no criticism, I wouldn't have minded, although, in the long run, it would have set me up for even more attachments, and I already had three. I was attached to Judaism being perfect, and I was attached to everyone recognizing that Buddhism is wonderful. I was also attached to my reputation.

Shantideva, a sixth-century Buddhist commentator, addresses the challenge of hearing criticism in *Guide to the Bodhisattva's Way of Life*. He asks, "Suppose someone disparages your 'good name'?" What I had inferred from my friend's relayed message about the overheard conversation was that "Sylvia isn't doing the right thing" or "Sylvia is making a mistake." If I had followed Shantideva's advice, I would have reflected, "Is that person correct? If her criticism is valid, I should accept it and change. Maybe even be grateful." Or, "Is that person incorrect? If her criticism isn't valid, there isn't a problem."

Either way it need not have been a problem and need not have caused suffering. What that person said was, after all, just an idea, something to think about. I should have remembered the second Noble Truth of the Buddha, the explanation of suffering as the *extra* tension in the mind in response to challenge, the tension of greed or aversion rather than the simplicity of clear, wise response. If my mind had not reacted with flurry to what it perceived as a challenge, the remark would have been a nonevent.

More Profound Is Not the Point

AT NAROPA INSTITUTE IN BOULDER, COLORADO, IN the early 1980s, I was one of eight faculty members at a Christian-Buddhist conference. I remember that Jim Finley, a psychotherapist from Southern California who had been a novice for some years at Gesthemene Monastery, in response to someone's earnest question— "Dr. Finley, why are you a Catholic?"—replied, "I am a Catholic because my mother was." When I recall his answer, I often recall Thomas Merton's entry in his *Asian Journal*, after a day of meeting with Buddhist teachers whom he admired: "And I'm *very* glad that I have Jesus."

Not long ago I was teaching in Barre, Massachusetts, with my friend Joseph Goldstein, and I told him I have become quite actively and happily and openly Jewish. He asked, "Do you believe that Judaism is as profound a religion as Buddhism?"

"I think it is," I said, talking fast and loud because we were on our way to teach a class together, and we were walking outdoors and it was February and it was snowing. Joseph has been one of my important Buddhist teachers, and his opinion of me matters. "There were many important Jewish thinkers who saw past the concept of God as Other, who had nondual understanding," I said, and mentioned Moshe Chaim Luzzato, whose writings (at least to me) often sound like something the Buddha might have said. I thought of naming some modern Jews, whose view of God, more philosophical than mystical, more emphasizing faith in the perfectibility of people than the perfection of a separate God, seems similar to my Buddhist view of the radiant, compassionate essence of natural mind.

Our conversation was cut short by the cold weather and the class we were teaching together. But later on, recalling it, I thought, "Joseph was just asking a question. I was defending myself and I didn't need to." More profound is not the point. I'm not a Jew because I figured out that Judaism is the wisest religious choice. Religion, I think, is a matter of the heart as much as, perhaps more than, a matter of the mind. Jim Finley's mother was a Catholic. Thomas Merton was glad that he had Jesus. Judaism feels right to me. Not *sounds* correct. Feels right.

Another Attachment Story

I TOLD MY FRIEND JOELLE, "I KNOW A VERY GOOD STORY that makes the point that attachment causes suffering. It's a Jewish story because it tells about the rabbis at my wedding, but I'm not sure it's in good taste. Some of the rabbis in the story look silly."

Joelle said, "Tell me the story. I'll tell you what I think. "

Seymour and I were married at a large, modern, conservative synagogue in Brooklyn on June 19, 1955. It was not our regular local *shul*. My parents chose the Madison Jewish Center because our next-door neighbor Joe Dornstein had the kosher catering franchise in that synagogue, and it had been understood since I was a child that whenever I married, the choice of synagogue would rest on where he had the catering concession.

My mother-in-law was eager to have the rabbi who had officiated at Seymour's bar mitzvah also officiate at his wedding. My family agreed, and so that rabbi called the Madison Jewish Center rabbi and announced his interest in being part of the ceremony. The resident rabbi agreed, adding, "Of course, since it's my pulpit, I'll need to be there as well. I'll just say the first prayer."

"That's no good," the bar mitzvah rabbi said, "that's the most important prayer."

The story we heard was that the resident rabbi replied, "If that's your attitude, you don't need to come at all."

Between their initial conversation and the wedding itself, there was a volley of phone calls, none of which apparently ended well.

The day before the wedding, the cantor of the synagogue phoned to reassure me, "I myself am an ordained rabbi," he said, "and I'm calling to tell you that in the event that these two other rabbis come to blows before the ceremony, I will officiate. You don't need to worry."

The cantor was an unforeseen rabbinic addition. One further unanticipated addition was Rabbi Avol, my father's uncle. David Avol had survived the war in Europe, although his family had not, and he, along with other relatives, had spent time in our home in Brooklyn en route to farmland given to them by the Canadian government in Saskatoon, Saskatchewan. I had met these relatives when I was nine years old. Ten years later my father invited them to my wedding, and, unexpectedly, they all arrived. They moved in with us in European *shtetl*-style for several days before the wedding.

At the Madison Jewish Center, just before the ceremony was about to begin, Uncle Avol, unaware of American rabbinic protocol, advised my father: "Nephew, it would give me a lot of pleasure to participate in your daughter's wedding."

Rabbi Avol said this in Yiddish, of course, since he spoke no English. The ceremony was about to start. My father did not have time to explain American customs. He confronted the rabbis and said: "This is my uncle, Rabbi Avol. He wants to be part of the ceremony."

The three rabbis were startled. They looked at Rabbi Avol, a little old man with a big beard and a frock coat who didn't speak English, and probably recognized intuitively that he could not have been *other* than a survivor of the war in Europe. I think the startle cleared their minds. All animosity disappeared. They handed Rabbi Avol the *ketubah* (the marriage contract), he officiated as Seymour and I signed it, and he read it in Aramaic during the ceremony. He looked very little and very old standing among the three tall, robust American rabbis.

When I told Joelle the Four Rabbis story, she said, "What does that prove?"

I said, "I just *now* understand it, forty-one years after the fact. All these years I thought it was just a cute story—a personal *Goodbye, Columbus* wedding story. I've never told it with malice—just as a silly story, and people always laughed. Now I see it's a Four Noble Truths story, *and* it's also a good example of the kindness and generosity of the natural mind when it isn't clouded by tension."

"Tell me both ways," Joelle said.

I said, "Well, here's the Four Noble Truths version. Here is the first Truth. Everything is impermanent, so nothing remains satisfactory. We were happy. The plans seemed fine. Then things changed and suddenly we were all suffering.

"The second Noble Truth is that the cause of suffering is attachment. The rabbis were attached to their roles, and they suffered. I was attached to their being civil to each other, and I suffered. I *could* have had another attitude. I could have thought, 'Far out, this may be an amazing wedding, and I might write a story about it someday.'

"The third Noble Truth is that nonattachment is freedom. At the zero hour, everyone dropped their attachments, and then no one suffered."

"What's the fourth Noble Truth?" Joelle asked.

"Well, actually the fourth truth is the practice path— Right Wisdom, Right Practice, and Right Behavior—that lessens attachment. The only way it fits into this story is by its notable absence. Most of us hadn't practiced enough!"

"What about the natural mind version?" Joelle asked.

"The natural mind," I replied, "is free of tensions and doesn't allow attachments to become entrenched. Preferences arise, but they dissipate without causing problems when the mind is relaxed. Annoyance also arises, but it doesn't take up residence. Fears and hurt feelings, doubts and desires, all come up in response to challenges and disappointments, but they don't linger. They don't upset basic clarity. The elegant expression for this," I said, is "'All defilements are self-liberating in the great space of awareness.'"

"What does that mean?" Joelle asked.

"It means 'all the nonsense falls out of your head when it's screwed on straight.'"

"You can't say that in a *book*," Joelle laughed.

"Maybe not," I replied, "but it's true."

The Possibility of Peace

THE THIRD NOBLE TRUTH OF BUDDHISM IS THE possibility of peace. Two insights into the possibility of peace were part of my first retreat experience. One was, in the realm of relative importance, quite trivial. The other was a life-and-death awareness. Both were valuable examples of the third Noble Truth of the Buddha, the possibility of not complicating pain with extra struggle.

The "trivial" instance was a response to an overheard casual remark that, had it happened five seconds earlier or five seconds later, I might have missed. It was an insight into *dukkha* (the extra struggle we create around the inevitable challenges of life). It had all the hallmarks of "insight"—it was startling, it was surprising, it offered a new perspective. The remark itself had to do, probably, with plumbing.

Somewhere in the middle of the retreat, the bell rang, marking the end of a period of sitting meditation. I had been struggling to keep my body and mind comfortable. The schedule was rigorous, and I was bewildered by the instructions. The teachers spoke about "clarity of intention," and I often didn't have it. I stood up, massaged my aching knees, and began to walk toward the door to begin a period of walking meditation. I passed the teacher just as the person in charge of retreat center logistics was delivering, in a whisper since we were all in silence, some message about a problem.

"Bzzz, bzzz, bzzz." Worried face. Furrowed brow.

The teacher thought for a moment, and then, in a very kind voice, said: "Look, I'm not into hassling . . . "

"Not hassling? That's an alternative!" I realized. "Another possible way to respond." I was surprised. I understood that the teacher was not being dismissive, that the problem would be addressed. But, without *extra* upset. A noncombative response, the Buddha taught, assures that pain does not become suffering. And, unclouded by the tension of struggle, the mind is able to assess clearly and respond wisely.

The nontrivial, life-and-death awareness came as the result of a phone call on the last evening of the retreat after the silence was ended. Ten minutes before the phone call, had anyone asked, "Are you at all changed by this practice?" I would have said, "I'm a *little* slowed down, and my sense perception is a *bit* sharper—I can smell the breakfast porridge all the way down the hall—but otherwise, I'm the same." Talking on the telephone, I knew I wasn't the same.

My phone call was to my husband, a routine call about my flight arrival time the next day. In response to my inquiring about my father, he said, "I'm sorry to tell you that your father has been diagnosed with an incurable cancer." This was unexpected bad news. My father was relatively young and vigorous and had been, until then, in fine health. I was very saddened by the news, but, uncharacteristically, I wasn't frightened. I thought, "I'm *so* sorry this is happening." I realized that I felt shock and grief *and* calm all at the same time. I hadn't known that was possible.

I've looked for the correct words to describe my experience.

Sometimes I've said, "The mind, free of tension, is spacious." Actually, the mind is *always* spacious—its essence is seamless spaciousness—tangles of tensions, the tensions of combative responses, cause it to *feel* constricted.

The tensions cause suffering. The tensions *are* suffering. For me, the word *soft* also works well. The mind free of tensions is soft. Malleable. It absorbs shocks. It uses the wisdom of insight to retain its ease. Shocks pass through it because they don't get caught in tangles. This is the image I have in mind when I say the prayer "*Ana B'choach . . .* " (Please, with Your great strength, untie my tangles . . .).

The years of my father's illness weren't terrible. There were painful events, but in between there were pleasant times. He and I heard Luciano Pavarotti sing Radames in *Aida* at the San Francisco Opera very near the end of his life. He said, "These tickets were very expensive. I'm glad I stayed alive long enough to use them!" My father's favorite prayer was "*Shehechiyanu . . .* " (thanksgiving for having been sustained in life until the present moment). He said it about expensive opera tickets. Also about the first asparagus every spring.

When I tell my "telephone call on my first retreat" story in a Buddhist context, I always say, "I'm so glad that I heard the news at just that time. Otherwise, two weeks earlier or two weeks later, in habitual tense mind, I might not have realized the potential of mindfulness." When I tell the story to Jews, I allow myself an extra elaboration. (I don't make it up for Jews—I already made it up for myself—I just feel comfortable *telling* Jews.) I say, "I have the feeling that God arranged for me to have the news of my father's cancer just at that time so I would notice the importance of mindfulness and dedicate myself to practice." With or without elaboration, I credit the telephone experience with being the event that most dedicated me to continued practice.

Silence Is a Fence for Wisdom

Pirkey Avot, Chapter III, Verse 17

INTENSIVE MINDFULNESS RETREAT PRACTICE SEEMS TO me a particular form of prayer. I tell students, "We have a liturgy of silence." Silence is a tool, a context for direct, personal, intuitive understanding of how things are. Silence isn't Buddhism, and it isn't mindfulness, but it is one aspect of what drew me and many others to Buddhist meditation practice. Its great overriding value is the support it provides for insight; its immediately evident value is, it's a relief!

I recall a question a student asked Jack Kornfield midway in a retreat very early in my own practice. The student was wearing clothing that identified her as a member of a religious community. She said, "This practice is so *dry*. No chanting. No ritual. Where is the *bhakti* (devotion) in this practice?" And Jack said, "I think this is the most *bhakti* practice of all. You sit down and say 'Here I am, God. Do whatever You want with me.'" Jack's answer informed my practice enormously. I understand it both as an instruction and as a wisdom teaching. Everything is manageable.

Silence supports paying close attention, which makes it possible to experience directly the truth of how things are. *Revelation* is a word I like a lot. I could hear—any number of times—that attachment causes suffering; until I experienced, directly, the pain of attachment and the freedom (nonpain) of nonattachment, I continued my mind habit of clinging. Hearing about liberation was inspiring, but my experience has been that I needed to *feel* trapped and *feel* free—over and over again—for change to begin to happen.

Being silent for me doesn't require being in a quiet place, and it doesn't mean not saying words. It means, "receiving in a balanced, noncombative way what is happening." With or without words, the hope of my heart is that it will be able to relax and acknowledge the truth of my situation with compassion.

I've discovered there are only two modes of the heart. We can struggle, or we can surrender. *Surrender* is a frightening word for some people, because it might be interpreted as passivity, or timidity. Surrender means wisely accommodating ourselves to what is beyond our control. Getting old, getting sick, dying, losing what is dear to us—what the Buddha taught as the first Noble Truth of life's unsatisfactoriness—is beyond our control. I can either be frightened of life and mad at life—or not. I can be *disappointed* and still not be mad. Stopping being mad—when I can—translates, for me, as being compassionate—to myself as well as to other people.

I became kinder by practicing mindfulness. I didn't begin my practice motivated by a wish to be kinder. I thought I was kind *enough*. I was motivated by fear. I was frightened by the fragility of life—what might happen to us, or to the people we loved. I was frightened when things—in my family, in my life, in the world—didn't go "my way" because I was sure that "my way" was right. I was attached, using Buddhist language, to my opinions. I was proud of my opinions. I called it "standing behind my convictions." I enjoyed saying, "I come from a long line of opinionated women."

Once, many years ago, I spent several weeks doing intensive mindfulness practice in a monastery in Massachusetts. In the weeks just prior to that retreat, the news media had followed the story of a young child with leukemia whose parents, dedicated to alternative healing, had refused to accept conventional treatment for him. The child had died. Since childhood leukemia has a high cure rate with modern medicines, I was very upset about what I considered the parents' "attachment to New Age views." I was more than upset—I was mad. "How could they do this?" I thought. I was mad, by extension, at everything that I associated with "New Age." I was mad at journals and books and diet regimens and health food stores—I was mad at anything I felt had colluded in the formation of these parents' attachment to a view I thought had cost the child his life. I also felt righteous in my anger since I was, at that time, a vegetarian, a yoga teacher, and a meditation practitioner, and I thought I had made my choices wisely while other people were being narrow-minded and rigid and thereby giving *my* choices a bad name.

I arrived at the retreat troubled by my anger, which I knew was obsessive, and which continued for days in spite of my attempts to develop composure. I'm fairly sure that the level of my anger was also sustained by my fear about what I considered inadequate parenting. I had young children of my own at the time, and the idea that parents might be so trapped by views that they could make decisions with dire consequences frightened me. Every time I remembered the story, my mind filled with anger and indignation. I began to feel additional anger, a resentment that these parents, strangers to me, had "destroyed my retreat by their behavior." I felt so burdened that I prayed that no reminder of the entire incident might arise in my mind to trigger another attack of anger.

One afternoon, sitting quietly, in a moment in which my mind was completely resting, an entirely new thought arose. "Those parents must be in *terrible* pain!" And then, "How are they going to *live* with themselves?" I was startled and *very* relieved to find all my anger was gone. I still thought the refusal of medicine was a wrong choice, but I felt sad in place of mad, and, finally, compassionate. "What if I made a terrible mistake—even a well-intentioned terrible mistake—with my children?" I thought. "I couldn't bear it."

At the moment of my change of heart I was so grateful—I felt like I'd escaped from an impossible, painful trap—that I didn't think about why or how it had happened. I was just glad to have been set free. It felt like a miracle.

Now I think I understand it. In fact, it's fundamental Dharma. The natural mind, unclouded by tension, reacts to pain with compassion. It just does. The mind confused by fear reacts to pain with aversion, and the bigger the fear, the more confusion, the more aversion. I think my prayer, "May I be *free* of this painful anger," was an expression of my suffering. The "miracle" that happened to me was that I sat long enough, with enough determination, with enough dedication to focusing my attention, to clear my mind long enough for its natural quality of compassion to manifest.

A Renewed Jew

SOME FRIENDS OF MINE, AWARE OF MY GREAT RESPECT
for Buddhist understanding and of my dedication to practice, have been surprised at my renewed interest in
Judaism. "Why," they wondered, "would you want to complicate yourself with Judaism?" It's not a question, for me,
of *deciding* to complicate myself with Judaism. I *am* complicated with Judaism. I have too much background in it not
to be. More important, though, is that the complication
nourishes me. I love it.

Ten years into my Buddhist meditation practice, five
years after I decided to get serious about cultivating concentration, many years after I knew for certain that ordinary
practice—plain mindfulness—relieved suffering, some un-
ordinary meditation experiences began to happen to me.
Years before, I had read Gopi Krishna's book *Kundalini,* in
which he described a sudden energy explosion in his body,
the result, he felt, of his meditation practice. He was over-
whelmed by the experience and required a long period of re-
cuperation and a special diet. I remember thinking, "I hope
that never happens to me." I also remembered conversations I'd had with my friend Mary Neill, a Dominican nun,
about the possible dangers of mystical experience. Mary had
given me an elegantly printed decorative card quoting St.
John of the Cross: "Lord, spare me visions." We had agreed
that the most reliable wisdom was ordinary clarity.

One day, in the middle of a meditation retreat, I felt my
eye tearing. "That's odd," I thought. "I'm not sad. Why am I
crying?" I reached up to wipe the tear away and discovered

that my face was dry. Soon my other eye was tearing. Soon my whole body was streaming with what I described to my teacher, Joseph Goldstein, as lines of energy.

"I feel like an acupuncture wall chart," I told him. "Those charts are true! We really *do* have energy bodies. We *are* energy bodies." I'd forgotten about my former disdain for mystical experiences. Suddenly I was interested. I started a diary of my experiences. Joseph was supportive and, correctly, I believe, unimpressed. "Just watch to see that you don't become captivated by it," he said. "It's just energy. It will pass. Don't let yourself become attached."

I'm not sure if his advice was too late and my energy system was, by that time, off and running by itself, or whether, in spite of his advice, I chose to let myself be captivated. I was completely enthralled by energy experiences that I could not have previously imagined. Whenever I sat still with my eyes closed, I felt as if I were vast space filled with "sparkles." I had no sense of the pressure of my body sitting, and no sense of limbs. Just space. Whenever I remembered my real life, it seemed like a story happening somewhere else. I thought, "I'm just an energy body, floating around, and I think I'm associated with *that* particular story, but probably I'm everyone's energy body and everyone's story." I thought, "I bet this is what people mean when they talk about mystical union." I didn't sleep for days.

My sense that I had stumbled into the same energy space as the mystics who wrote Genesis started suddenly with a powerful burst in the center of my forehead. I felt filled with light, in fact, *saw* bright light, all with my eyes closed. I was ecstatic. The phrase "And God said, 'Let there be light,' and there was light, and God saw that the light was good" arose in my mind. I thought, "It's about the be-

ginning of consciousness, not the beginning of the world."
I imagined meditators in caves in prebiblical times having
my same experiences and thinking, "How can I tell this as
a story?"

Periods of intense light came and went, and in between,
my experience was one of vast spacious mind. I felt that
thoughts, ideas, even sounds were energy winds that blew
through me. I *felt* them move through as sparkling showers. Thoughts and sounds were indistinguishable from
each other. "This is what it means," I thought, "when it
says, 'spread out the firmament.'" From time to time, a
clear thought, an identifiable perception, would arise in my
mind. "And this," I thought, "is all the rest of creation—
everything in its particularity." I marveled at how creation
was always happening. Out of a formless void, out of vast
space, distinct objects—thoughts, perceptions, body sensations—would present themselves and then disappear. I
thought of the Mahayana Buddhist teaching, "Form is
emptiness and emptiness is form," and I thought of the
first line of the *Dhammapada*, "Mind is the author of all
things." Mostly I thought, "In the beginning, God created
heaven and earth."

I began to recognize how each new energy play would
link itself to Hebrew Scripture image. I felt that my mind
was writing captions to describe experiences. I would feel
suddenly engulfed by energy, and I would think, "This is
the flood . . . Now the flood waters are receding . . . Now
creation is beginning again." I spent some days attending
to what felt like a line being drawn, in energy, down the
length of my body, as if someone were dividing me into
two halves with an invisible laser. "This is the Adam and
Eve story," I thought. I was excited about that idea. Then, I

thought, "If I'd had a different background, I would be thinking, 'This is how people came to use yin/yang imagery.' But I don't have another background. I have *my* background. That's why I have *this* imagery, *these* phrases to label experience, and *these* interpretations. I am a Jew."

Some days later, I awoke from a nap with the distinct feeling that someone was in bed with me, breathing on me. Startled, I opened my eyes. I was alone. "Maybe it's me breathing," I thought. "Maybe I'm feeling my own breath." I held my breath. The sense of being breathed on continued—firmly, rhythmically. I felt excited and peaceful at the same time. First I thought, "And the spirit of God moved on the face of the waters." Then, I thought, "God is breathing on me. I am in the presence of God, and God is breathing on me."

I was seeing my teacher for daily interviews during that practice period and in our next meeting I told him my news. I described how this new experience, one that I called "presence," had continued through walking periods, mealtimes, sitting meditation, even my salad-making "work meditation."

"God is breathing on me," I told him.

"Be careful, Sylvia," he replied, smiling. "Don't reify."

"Thanks," I said. "I'll be careful."

That particular energy experience continued for some weeks. I told Joseph about my experience, but I didn't tell him about my elaborations. I thought about them a lot, though. I also thought about my life and my family, and what had been, until then, problems that I worried about. I was amazed to discover that worries didn't get stuck in my mind the way they usually did. It wasn't that I didn't care about these problematic situations—I *did* care—and I knew

I would devote myself to solutions when I returned home. I just couldn't *worry*. The experience was so unusual for me that I laughed aloud in amazement when I heard myself think, "What if I *forget* how to worry?" As if that would be a problem! Worrying, fearfulness about the fragility, the un-predictability of life, *was* my problem. It was as if I had the worry, "What if I accidentally became enlightened?"

The altered energy experiences that began in the context of intensive meditation practice changed, over time, from pleasant and inspiring to unpleasant and disturbing. They continued outside of retreats and without any effort on my part to develop focused concentration. My sense of comfort-ing presence was replaced by despair that my body had been taken over by an energy beyond my control. My limbs would vibrate or spasm in random movements in public places, and sometimes I would awaken in the middle of the night to find my teeth chattering. My actual body tempera-ture stayed normal, while I experienced periods of shiver-ing with cold or imagining that I was radiating heat. When I felt sharp pains around my heart, I consulted my in-ternist, Martin Brotman.

"Do you ever have headaches?" he asked, beginning what I recognized as the standard inquiry into *all* the organ systems.

"Before we begin, I need to tell you," I said, "that *every-thing* about me feels peculiar these days. I've been meditat-ing quite a lot, and sometimes odd things happen to meditators."

Martin was wonderful. He never said, "Why do you meditate if it produces this kind of discomfort?" He said, "Your health is fine. And I'm interested in what's happen-ing to you. Let me know."

Three things happened. The unusual energy settled down. My understanding of suffering increased. And I began to read Scripture, and finally prayers, with new interest.

It took three or four years for my body to relax enough so that I could trust it to sleep at night and stay still in public places. I think the experience of dramatic physical sensations left me with an enhanced sense of vibrancy, a sensual liveliness that I enjoy and that pleases me. I'm convinced, though, that hatha yoga and t'ai chi also develop liveliness, less disruptively. I'm also sure that the energetic route my practice followed is not a *necessary* one for developing insight. Some people become wise very gently, just by paying attention. Sometimes, when I saw that happening to my friends, I envied them. Then, of course, I had the extra pain, the suffering, of envy.

I learned a lot about suffering from my energy experiences, even when they were pleasant. When they were pleasant, I immediately amplified their pleasantness (unconsciously, of course) by making up stories about them. Joseph had been correct. I *had* been reifying. I *liked* my reifications. They sustained me. Had I believed that God—as Other—was *really* breathing on me, was actually the cause of my feeling safe—I would have felt betrayed and abandoned when my experience became tedious.

I especially learned about suffering during the years of uncomfortable energy. I wanted *very* much for my experiences to end. Part of that was normal, of course, the natural aversive response of the mind to unpleasantness. In addition, I compounded my discomfort, once again, by telling myself stories. "This is all my fault," I would think. "I wasn't careful. I got seduced by pleasure, and I wanted even more. So this is like the Sorcerer's Apprentice—I asked for more and I got too much more." Curiously, now that I think about it, I never thought, "God is punishing me for my desire." I thought, "*I* am responsible for this distress; I have poisoned myself with desire." I remembered times, sitting on my *zafu* (meditation cushion), feeling filled with light, convinced that the cosmos and I were one seamless whole made up of vast space and twinkling stars, thinking, "Is this *all*?"

"It's *my* fault!" I said to myself. "I wanted too much." I never said, "It's God's fault."

I knew, at least consciously, that my various pains were being exacerbated by my struggles to end them. I tried not to struggle. I struggled anyway. I phoned a *kundalini* energy expert, who said, "This sort of stuff doesn't usually happen to people doing mindfulness meditation." I consulted an acupuncturist who said, "I see this fairly often," and prescribed herbs and acupuncture. The acupuncture relieved the energy intensity, at least temporarily, but the idea that I was being treated for something increased my sense of having a sickness. Also, the herbs were bitter. My friend Jack Kornfield said, "Eat heavier foods and make love more often." I tried, but I was usually too distracted to deal with regular appetites.

I made an appointment for an interview with Chagdud Rimpoche, a Tibetan lama who was temporarily in Berkeley. I was excited about the prospect of meeting him, and I remember my body vibrating as I drove across the Richmond Bridge for the interview. I was hoping he would cure me. I think I was also hoping that he would, at the very least, be impressed with what a good meditator I was.

I felt calmer as soon as I was in Chagdud's presence. He smiled at me as I told my whole story, and then he said, "How much compassion practice do you do every day?"

I was surprised. I had expected technical meditation instructions. I put together a makeshift, textbook answer about compassion being the inevitable fruit of wisdom.

"No, really," Chagdud said, "How much compassion practice do you do every day?"

"I'm not sure what you mean," I replied.

"You ought to go out into the street every day," he said, "and look around to see how much suffering there is."

I wasn't sure of the intent of Chagdud's instruction. We spoke through an interpreter, and my interview time was nearly up. "I wonder if Chagdud thinks I'm too self-centered," I thought, "that I have too much ego investment in this whole business." I considered feeling humiliated, but he seemed so benevolent. If he had thought I had too much ego, he had thought it without judgment. It was just a thought. "Maybe he's right," I decided, "but still, what should I *do*? Go in the street and notice the pain and do *what*?"

I told Chagdud I was considering spending a month in Barre doing *metta* (lovingkindness) practice.

"I don't think you should do that," he said. "It's more intense concentration practice. You'll probably increase all that energy."

I went to Barre anyway. *Metta* practice is concentration practice, but it's also a response to the awareness of suffering. Meditators begin by sensing their own suffering and their own deep desire for peace, for happiness. One technique of practice is the recitation of resolves: "May I be happy. May I be peaceful. May I be free of suffering." As practice proceeds, wishes for the peace and happiness of others replace wishes for oneself.

I discovered that Chagdud had been correct about the effects of intensive *metta* practice. Saying the resolves resolutely *did* amplify my energy states. So, I changed my practice style. I said resolves slowly, softly, sweetly—I sang the resolves to myself—and everything calmed down.

I spent several weeks in Barre, feeling as if I had been granted a reprieve. Sometimes I felt selfish because I sang resolves mostly for myself. From time to time, I'd think of the people I loved and sing some wishes for them—but not often and not for long. A few rounds of good thoughts for my family, and I'd find myself focused back on myself. I thought, "This is okay. This is true. The only pain and the only suffering I can *actually* feel is my own. This is real, Sylvia. Just do it."

As part of my intensive *metta* practice, my teacher Sharon Salzberg had me recite to myself, as a prelude to the traditional resolves, a ritual formula of preparation:

> People who practice *metta* sleep peacefully,
> wake peacefully, dream peaceful dreams.
> People love them. *Devas* [angels] love them.
> Devas will protect them.
> Poison and weapons and fire won't harm them.
> Their faces are clear, their minds are serene,
> They die unconfused, and, when they die,
> Their rebirth is in the Brahma realms.

I said the preparation formula a lot. I said it even though I sometimes had bad dreams and I always thought poison and weapons and fire would harm me. Sometimes, since *metta* is fundamentally a concentration practice and the formal "*metta* resolves" are one of a variety of possible objects of concentration, I *only* said the preparation. I would repeat it to myself with the same calm and focused dedication I brought to the resolves. I discovered it was steady concentration that cultivated happiness, not the words I chose to say.

As weeks passed, and as I felt increasingly healed of my energy crisis, I began to think about my family more. And my friends. And the woman across the hall who banged her door too loudly. After a while I even began to feel kindly toward her. I thought, "She must be *really* in pain, seriously distracted, to be banging so loudly." Then I thought, "*This* is compassion practice. When I'm confused by suffering, I'm unkind, even to myself. When I'm *not* suffering, I don't need to try to be compassionate. I just am."

The most obvious enduring sequelae of my "mystical imagery" energy experiences—obvious in the sense that I've made some life changes other people might notice—are my renewed enthusiasms for Jewish practices. I had started saying prayers—blessings of thanksgiving mostly—early in my practice. Indeed, as soon as I felt easier in my life, happier—which came *before* my energetic journey—I discovered my impulse to praise. *After* the energy-imagery experience—without a conscious plan—I began to read the Torah again, really for the first time with grown-up eyes. First I read randomly. At some point, I aligned myself with the calendar Torah portion. My interpretations are usually in terms of Dharma insights.

I never imagined that God, in the sense of any separate thing, was actually breathing on me. I was glad, though, that I had the *idea* that God was breathing on me because the *idea* sustained me. It was a personal shorthand for say-

ing, "the focused, alert mind—the undistracted, unconfused mind—is completely safe." In moments of presence I
am fearless. My Jewish shorthand is the last line of the
hymn *Adon Olam*, "God is with me; I am not afraid."

I was grateful—I *am* grateful—for my God imagery.
The years of peculiar, altered energy were difficult ones for
me. Whatever excitement I had ("I'm a special meditator
having special, exotic experiences.") was overshadowed by
concern ("I'm never going to be regular again. I can't be
comfortable in a public place! I am exhausted by this empty
energy display!"). I would return, as a way of steadying myself, to my memory of what it felt like to have "God breathing on me." It was my lifeline to mindfulness, to presence.
When I remembered to use it, I would feel safe again.

I never thought that my Scripture-image "revelations"
were other than mythic. Indeed, a great pleasure was thinking that they *were* mythic—and that my myths matched
those of particular mystics meditating a long time ago. I am
sure that truth is universal and that the stories that pass
that truth on through generations vary because we have different tribal lineages.

The fact that we *create* stories to pass on our best wisdom seems normal to me. We are a storytelling species. We
make up myths out of our experience, imbue them with
importance, *insist* that they teach us, and continue to find
them meaningful and useful. It pleases me to think that
every thirteen-year-old celebrant offering an interpretation
of the weekly Torah portion is contributing at that moment
the most contemporary addition to a living religion.

Not Quite Beyond Words

IN A TELEPHONE CONVERSATION WITH MY FRIEND
Thubten Chodren, a Jew who has been a Tibetan Buddhist
nun for twenty years, I mentioned that these days I am
often called upon to teach meditation to Jews. I said that
my own Judaism had been substantially enlivened by my
Buddhist practice. She asked, "What do you say to people
when they ask if you believe in God?"

I replied, "I say, 'Yes.'"

Chodren said, "That's great. I'll give you the name of a
friend of mine in Chicago, a Jew who has been my friend
since childhood. She's looking for a meditative path that
will connect her more with her Judaism."

I thought, "Good for Chodren!" She didn't say more. She
didn't ask, "How can you . . . ?", which presumes and challenges. She didn't even ask what, for me, is the best question—"What is your experience of God?"—and I'm glad.

I could have responded—an elegant enough, true
enough, Buddhist enough answer—"I experience God as
Source, the Emptiness that gives rise to Form." It isn't a
helpful answer though, unless I say "how" or "why." It isn't
a telephone answer.

I told a friend recently, "I'm having trouble writing
about God. I'd like to leave God out of the book. I can't exactly do that, though, because it's a book about being a
prayerful person, so I need to say something. I'd like to say,
'the tao that can be told isn't the eternal Tao,' which would
convey my meaning of God being beyond words. Maybe," I
said, "I could quote Psalm 65—'For you, silence is

praise'—as the Jewish equivalent of the Tao that cannot be spoken . . . talking about God is too hard!"

"You don't need to talk about God," my friend said. "You just need to talk about your *experience* of God. Go ahead. Do it. It will be easier than you think."

"Oh! Okay," I said. "I can do that. Thanks."

This is my experience. In periods of intensive meditation practice, at times when I have been very, very still, I've seen the world I know and recognize as myself and my story dissolve and become the vibrancy of infinite space. "Recognizing" is the right word to use to describe what *stops* happening. As attention becomes focused, the habitual reflexive movements of the attention in response to stimuli become steadier, calmer; the tendency to cognize— to name things—diminishes. Things are just things. Life becomes deconstructed. Textbooks call it "bare attention." The place from which—or perhaps it's better to say, the process by means of which—the sentient, discriminating awareness of life begins, is revealed. It feels to me like the edge of creation. I know the moments that approach that edge and I know the moments just after. The approach is now familiar to me. If I spend some days in silence, sitting still for significant periods of time, the neuronal synapse- leaps that string stories together stop happening. My experience is *just* sounds. *Just* sensations. *Just* smells. *Just* sights. *Just* tastes. *Just* thoughts. Plain. Not *boring*—plain. Actually amazingly plain. "Look at that! Basic building blocks of experiences, and every moment, with memory and cognition, I can remember myself!"

Or, I can choose not to. I can stay, by paying close and calm attention, at the level of just experience. Being still and being alert. Discrete, identifiable experiences come and go in the space of awareness. "There's a thought. I know it clearly. Now it vanishes." "There's a sound. I know it. It disappears." The mind is completely peaceful and alert. The sense of a *personal* "I"—some*one* who is having experiences—also disappears, but observing "here-ness" remains.

Complete here-ness is completely restful, completely safe, and endlessly fascinating. My experience can be, in one moment, bubbles of thought that burst into showers of sounds that echo into space, and in the next moment, a full appreciative recollection of Sylvia's particular story right now. My life remembers itself. I think to myself, "God is remembering me."

I feel, in moments of balanced here-ness, that I have binocular vision. I can look into the emptiness of undifferentiated Mind and know it as Source. I can look at elaborated Mind and see it as creation and know that everything, absolutely everything, is God in temporal, particular form. Looking at emptiness, I feel I see God. Looking at form, I feel like Adam, naming. And from that vantage point of balanced presence, God as Source and God as Form are inseparable. They are one. Nothing else exists. *Eyn Ode.* Nothing else.

I don't live in direct realization of nondifferentiated consciousness very often. Hardly ever, really. It's an altered mind awareness, and I know how to achieve it, but it isn't a big enough allure for me to take time to reside in it regularly. Anyway, no matter how still the mind becomes, no matter how long experience is deconstructed, eventually the whole world of phenomena begins again. Form is the manifest side of emptiness. Creation keeps on happening. I don't need to see the emptiness side directly if I know that the form side is its reflection.

Besides, I like the form side. In moments of clarity I know that I *need* the form side, I need my life and its story, in order to feel astonished. Discovering myself a participant—an engaged, emotional participant—in a world of lives born of the interaction of consciousness with the raw material of sense impression is, sometimes, beyond words.

I have had the impulse, sitting still somewhere, meditating at two o'clock in the morning, of suddenly wanting to kneel, or bow, or lie on the ground. Since most of my meditation practice has been in Catholic monasteries, that impulse retrieves my whole personal story. "What are you even *thinking* of, Sylvia? This is a church!"

My mind, balancing startle—surprised by intensity—invents a story. "Probably you felt that impulse because so many people, for so many years, have been kneeling in here beseeching God with prayer. It's the vibration in the room!" I know that's not true. The impulse is not in the room. The impulse is in me. And it isn't beseeching. When I feel like falling down, it is in complete gratitude.

My experience is a meditation experience. It's an experience that feels sacred, one that needs only to have happened once for my life to be informed by it forever. I wouldn't say, as a four-year-old boy in a yoga class I taught years ago did, "I saw God." I would say, "This is the closest I can come to describing my experience of God as the Source of all creation. This is not the God I 'believe in.' This is the God I know and trust with all my heart."

I thought this would be hard to write about, but it wasn't. It's not that I can't describe my experience. It's that I've had the concern, "If I say this out loud, maybe it will disappear. This is the most precious understanding I have. This is what sustains my life." But it doesn't disappear. My meditation experience happens in silence, but it is not beyond words. And my impulse to bow, whether or not bowing happens, does have words. "I love you."

Emptiness

EMPTINESS IS A BUDDHIST DESCRIPTION OF EXPERIENCE that sometimes worries people because it seems to imply that life is worthless. Perhaps the nihilistic ring of the word *emptiness* is confusing. My experience of emptiness is that it is alive with the possibility of everything waiting to be born. For me, emptiness means that all of creation *and* the source of creation is a seamless whole.

Buddhists say, "Form is emptiness and emptiness is form." Everything derives from and returns to its undifferentiated source. And there is nothing apart from that source. The Kabbalists call God *"Eyn-Sof,* the Infinite, that which has no beginning or end." The author of Job, speaking in nondual mind, as the Voice from the Whirlwind, sounds like a Buddhist.

Suzuki Roshi, founder of the San Francisco Zen Center, reassured his students in the last days of his life. "If, when I die, I seem to be suffering, do not be alarmed. That's just Suffering-Buddha-nature." The Chasidic master, Rebbe Zusya of Hanipol, questioned by his students about his painful, terminal illness, insisted he was not suffering. "I am happy. Zusya is happy to live in the world that God, may He be blessed, created."

I think a lot about a prayer that appears in the *Shacharit* (morning service) in some, but not all, of my *siddurim* (prayer books). It begins, "What are we? What is our life? What is our virtue . . . ?" and ends, "For the preeminence of humans over animals is illusory because everything is *havel*." *Havel* is translated in most of my sources as "vanity," but I prefer my Hirsch *siddur* translation of "insubstantial." Recognizing insubstantiality is the key to realizing the interconnectedness of all creation. When I say this prayer, I think of how "God is One" and "Emptiness" feel the same to me.

I told my friend Miles, "Every time I read that prayer I think, 'See, here is the teaching on emptiness.' Doesn't everyone read it that way?"

He said, "No, I don't think so. If you see it, you see it everywhere. If you don't, you don't get it by reading." I like to imagine, though, that it's one of those important phrases that incline the mind in the direction of truth.

When I give thanks, daily, for my life, I think about creation as the amazing process by which nondifferentiated emptiness continually is reborn as form. My consciousness refocuses from undifferentiated, sleeping form to my personal, familiar world. I remember who I am. Some of my most precious moments of insight have been those in which I have seen clearly that gratitude is the only possible response. In those moments I *know* that every single thing that ever happened in the cosmos needs to have happened for my life to be exactly what it is now. That everything that is manifest now cannot be anything but seamlessly interdependent and endlessly regenerative.

To myself, I say, "God reigns, God reigned, God will reign, forever."

To my grandchildren, I say, "Everything, no matter what, is okay. And we'll try as hard as we can to fix anything that's broken."

To Buddhist students, I say: "The cosmos is lawful. Karma is true. Everything evolves from a single interconnected source. Nothing is disconnected from anything else. Future events are dependent on our actions now. Virtue is mandated; we are responsible for one another. *Everything* matters."

Karma Is True

I EXPERIENCE THE COSMOS AS ALL-POWERFUL AND
compassionately embracing. I am certain that karma is the
lawful, relational dynamism of a seamlessly interconnected
infinite system that, because it is singular, cannot be arbi-
trary. I am surprised, now that I see it so clearly, that it took
me so long to say "I am sure."

I think traditional karma stories may have been the
principal deterrent to my understanding karma because
they are morality fables. "Just for *that*, you get this."
Circumstances are presented as rewards or punishments
for past actions rather than simply the *result* of actions. No
one "deserves" a holocaust, or an earthquake, or illness, or
being born into poverty. The idea that special extra pain in
life is the balance due on a specific former transgression
and that the debt might cost as much as a life never seemed
correct to me. It did not match my experience of life or my
sense of God.

My son Peter was born hard of hearing. I'd had the flu
early in my pregnancy with him and that seemed a likely
cause. Some years later I read a Buddhist karma treatise that
advised giving alms to monks to assure that your children
be born with perfect vision and perfect hearing. I didn't believe it. I decided the treatise had been written by a worried
monk not yet ready to rely on natural generosity. I could not
imagine that Peter's hearing loss was the result of one moment of nongenerosity in anyone's life. Besides, Peter's
hearing wasn't a *problem* in our lives. His teachers loved

him. "He really pays attention," they said. We didn't think of his hearing as a "bad" thing or a "good" thing. It was just a *thing*. I couldn't believe retributive karma stories because, apart from context, everything is a *thing*.

I was talking to my friend Miles on the telephone about karma stories. He told me a story from the Talmud about Nachum of Gamzu.

Nachum of Gamzu, revered by his students as their rebbe, had neither arms nor legs, only stumps. His body was covered with boils. What's more, he was blind in both eyes. Nevertheless, his demeanor was so loving and saintly that an air of protection surrounded him.

"How could this have happened to you?" his students asked.

"Earlier in my life," Nachum responded, "I was traveling to visit my father-in-law. I was leading donkeys whose saddle bags were filled with good food and drink. On the way, I was stopped by a desperately poor person who begged me for sustenance. I told him to wait while I unpacked the saddle bags. Before I offered food, the man died. My eyes had not perceived his pain quickly enough, my body did not feel his pain quickly enough, my arms and legs did not move quickly enough. From that time I've been just as you see me now."

"Woe to us to see you this way," Nachum's students said.

"No. Woe to me if you didn't see me this way," Nachum responded.

I said, "I think this must be a teaching story, Miles, that catches the attention because it's so dramatic. The part about Nachum's drastic physical karma is extra. Genuine remorse is enough. I think the main point is that his students loved and revered him because he was completely benevolent."

I told Miles the story of Angulimala, a notorious murderer whose name means "finger garland." Through a misunderstanding, Angulimala had become convinced that he needed to kill one thousand people in order to win his teacher's favor. After each murder, he removed one of the victim's fingers and strung them into a necklace which he wore around his neck. Angulimala had already murdered 999 people in a rampage of killing when he met the Buddha, whom he was intent to have as his thousandth victim. The Buddha, with his omniscient power, was able to continue his serene walk while so confounding Angulimala's understanding that Angulimala was unable to catch him. Finally, Angulimala called out in dismay, "Stop! Stop!" The Buddha replied, "I stopped a long time ago. When will you stop?"

Angulimala stopped. He instantly understood the serenity that came from renouncing violence and joined the Buddha's order of monks. During alms rounds, people who recognized him threw stones at him and wounded him. Angulimala remained steadfastly serene and performed acts of great compassion and ultimately became fully enlightened. After I finished telling about Angulimala, I said, "You know, Miles, both stories seem gratuitously gruesome. I'll think about this."

I've decided—this is my most spacious view—that both stories are awkward attempts to teach morality. I wonder if they are useful. I think they condition incredulity rather than inspire kindness. I'm also concerned they might be interpreted as demanding passive acceptance of fate. The important message of both stories—a benevolent heart is the ultimate refuge—is hidden in horror. I want to teach karma by amazing, not by frightening, because that's the way I learned.

My preliminary glimpses of the truth of karma happened, as insights do, over many years of practice and always in the context of a relaxed and focused mind. My fullest understanding began as I was teaching a class at Spirit Rock Meditation Center. I was saying, "I wish I understood karma more fully. I am sure of proximal karma but I'm not clear about the meaning of karma over lifetimes." Then I said, "If my grandson Erik sneezes on me and I develop a cold, my cold will be the karmic consequence of our being together, but it will not be a reflection of any conduct *other* than my being in the line of fire of his sneeze."

Then the next thing I said was "Of course, in order that Erik, in every cell of his particularity, be exactly where he is when he sneezes and for me, in all my particularity, to be where I am at that moment requires that the entire cosmos has to have unfolded exactly as it did." As I heard myself, I *knew* it was true. I felt it. I stopped, surprised. I told my class, "I'm quite startled. I *am* sure of karma over lifetimes. I *just* saw it."

When I reconstructed that moment afterward, I recalled visualizing myself and Erik together. As I said the words "In order for us to be there in our particularity," the faces of my parents and Erik's parents joined the image in my mind of the two of us. And, as I said, "to be exactly where each of us is," the immediate image of six people cracked kaleidoscopically into an infinite, intricate, collaborative connection of all ancestors and all actions and all ages forever and ever, and I absolutely know now that Erik sneezing depends on the totality of creation. It cannot be otherwise.

In the days that followed I couldn't *not* see the truth of karma. It was everywhere. I was thrilled. The least important benefit of that realization is that it freed me from having to say, "I'm a Buddhist teacher but I don't get it about karma." The most important is my confidence that nothing happens that isn't completely correct. "God in His wisdom, He is right," my grandmother's Purim song, is true. "Blessed is God, . . . the true Judge," the blessing said upon receiving sad news, is the parachute for catching the mind from crashing in pain and forgetting that a just cosmos is perfectly precise. The Buddhist equanimity meditation "Every individual is heir to their own karma" has nothing to do with atoning or reaping rewards. What we inherit, uniquely, is the totality of a completely lawful cosmos. Erik's sneeze is the great-great-great-great grandchild of the moment of creation, it is a relative of the stars, and it is part of the legacy of the world to come.

I phoned a close friend and said, "I'm so excited about what I see that I'm shaking and my knees are wobbly. I'm lying on the floor so I can talk to you."

"Lying on the floor is okay," he said. "Tell me what you know."

"I know what *Gam zu l'tova* (This also is for the good) means," I said. "It doesn't mean, 'this painful situation is going to end up gratifying.' Sometimes things get better. Sometimes they get worse. *Gam zu l'tova* means that creation is good and the divine orderliness of creation is good and *everything* is good. Not *for* the good, just good."

After I hung up the phone I thought for a while about "Everything is foreseen, yet freedom is given" (*Pirkey Avot,* chapter III, verse 19). At first I thought, "Okay, every moment is determined by what has been, but I am free to choose a response." Then, remembering how everything arises according to conditions, including my intentions, I began to wonder about how free my will actually was. I started shaking again. Then I remembered the cosmic echo of Erik's sneeze, realized the limitless effect of every action through all time and space, and I shook even more.

I phoned my friend again and said, "I've been insisting that *yirah* means 'awe,' not 'fear,' but I think I might be wrong. My current understanding has no slack in it. Incarnation seems like a trap. We need to act, but every move is so responsible. Everything matters. I know I must be missing something," I said, "but I don't know what it is yet. I do know," I added, "what 'God hears the bells on the ankle bracelet of an ant' means. I never understood that before."

Two days later at Shabbat services, I heard a particular phrase tucked into the middle of the rabbi's discussion of *Parashat Chukat* (the Red Cow) and I thought, "That's the answer." He had been talking about whether the miracle of water in the desert had been "the merit of Miriam" or "the merit of Abraham," and suggested that since Miriam was Abraham's descendant, both she and her merit were Abraham's merit as well. In that moment I realized that everyone's merit is everyone's merit and everyone's confusion is also everyone else's. I immediately recalled a line from a Talmud teaching, "Whoever saves a single soul saves the whole world," and the bodhisattva pledge "I vow to end all suffering," and I understood them both. We *are* alive, and we *do* need to act, and nothing less than impeccability of intention is required. But also nothing more. I can do that.

I thought for a long time, trying to understand karma, and so thinking was one of the conditions for insight arising. So were the moments of intention practice I did daily. "May the clearest understanding of karma I've ever had arise in my mind today." Another condition was the energetic interest of my students at Spirit Rock, whose confidence in me allowed me to be completely at ease when I said, "I don't fully understand karma . . ." My hearing the Torah discussion of the Red Cow was another conditioning event, and that event depended on my paying attention as well as on the lives of the Spanish missionaries who founded the city of Santa Rosa. Not all conditions have equal weight, of course, and proximal conditions often seem most significant—but *everything* counts. How could I have missed seeing that for so long? And how could I have imagined that fear is any part of it? There is nothing but awe, no relief from unremitting back-to-back moments of awe, and no possible response but praise.

Halleluya. Praise God.

Permission and Inspiration

SEYMOUR'S COUSIN MARTIN PHONED FROM NEW YORK
when he heard we were planning a trip to Jerusalem.

"Please visit Rabbi Mordechai Sheinberger," he said.
"You can convey my respects personally, and I'd appreciate
that. Besides, I think it might be wonderful for you. When I
first met him, ten years ago, he completely reinspired me,
turned my life around. Here's his address."

"Okay," we said. "We'll do it."

Seymour and I arrived in Jerusalem on a Thursday, and
the next morning we located Rabbi Sheinberger's apartment in the Old City.

Seymour said, "Let's go up and introduce ourselves."

I hesitated. "I don't think it's a good idea," I said, "to
visit *erev* (the day before) Shabbat."

Seymour prevailed.

"We'll just say 'Hello.' It'll be fine."

I let Seymour ring the bell. Rabbi Sheinberger answered
and expressed delight—"Any cousin of Martin Boorstein is
a friend to me already"—and invited us in. His wife looked
out from the kitchen and smiled a welcome. Rabbi
Sheinberger gestured us toward the large dining table that
also serves as class meeting table for his weekly *shi'urim*
(discourses). He sat at the head of the table, and Seymour
sat to his right. I took a seat at the foot of the table, the far-
thest away. In all of our subsequent visits, I never saw a
woman even sit at that table. I had dressed in my Jerusalem
costume—long dress, long sleeves, hair-covering hat. I sat

quietly, the men spoke. The conversation was cordial, generic.

"How is Martin Boorstein?"

"He is very well. He sends respectful regards."

"How long will you be in Jerusalem?"

"Four weeks."

"Very good. Come for *kiddush* (blessing and sharing of wine) after the *davven*ing (prayer service) tomorrow morning and stay afterward to eat with us."

Soon, all *too* soon I thought, Seymour said, "My wife Sylvia here is a Buddhist meditation teacher." I thought, "You could have *waited* before making that announcement." The next moment was for me a defining one.

Rabbi Sheinberger leaned forward. "What do you teach?" he asked. "Whom do you teach? How do you teach? What have you learned from your own meditations?" And, "Tell me about the most difficult time you ever had with meditation."

In five minutes I was telling Rabbi Sheinberger an account of my confusing years of strange rapture energy, partly in English, partly in Yiddish when I felt I could make it more clear to him. Then he said, "Well, I'm not a meditation teacher, but this is what I think. I think you did too much rapture practice. A little rapture every day is good for you. Maybe two hours a day. More than that is not balanced. The rest of the time you should have been bringing the rapture into your life, into being with people."

I was thinking, "This is a terrific meditation interview. He's right. [By that time I knew the right answer, too.] I can't think of any Buddhist teacher I know who would have done this interview better or would have known a more correct answer."

Rabbi Sheinberger ended by saying, "But I'm not a meditation teacher. I teach the path of *mitzvot* (mandated observance)." He suggested that I read Moshe Chaim Luzzato's *The Path of the Just*. I bought the book that day, read it the next day, and went back on Sunday to talk further.

Clearly, the path of *mitzvot* is a form of meditation. The intention to act impeccably requires complete dedication and unwavering attention. I was impressed when I read *The Path of the Just* with how clearly it presents *mitzvot* practice as the path to clear seeing. I was also impressed with Luzzato's insistence that *mitzvot* practice is joyful.

In Buddhism, it is called *sila* (virtue) practice. *Sila* practice was first explained to me as preparation practice for meditation. It was presented as a sensible way to live *if* a person wanted to meditate. I was taught that Right Effort, Right Concentration, and Right Mindfulness—the path components specially designed as meditative—are easier to establish when the mind is free of guilt. That's true, of course, but it's also true in reverse order.

The three *sila* components of the Buddha's Eightfold Path are morality instructions: Right Action, Right Speech, and Right Livelihood. Although there are precise instructions for all three categories and extensive commentary and interpretation as well, they all can be understood as a dedication to action that is not motivated by greed or anger or confusion. The Buddha advised practitioners to reflect before *every* action, "Is what I am about to do for the good of others as well as for myself?" He further advised that the same scrutiny be maintained during as well as after an action. If, at any time, self-serving motivation becomes apparent, a course correction can be made and the action amended before, or during, or even after its completion.

It seems completely clear to me that *sila* practice mandates effort, concentration, and mindfulness. Right Effort, the Buddha taught, is the effort to notice the painful presence of anger, greed, and confusion in the mind. The process of noticing lessens their power. Right Effort also includes noticing the *pleasant* presence of loving, compassionate feelings so that they become habitual. Right Effort conditions (that's a Buddhist word—it means *leads* to) virtuous action.

Right Concentration—keeping the mind composed and focused—is an essential part of Right Mindfulness, the capacity of mind to understand current experience completely and clearly. Actions born of mindful clarity are kind and compassionate. Remembering the particulars of an ethics code is not necessary. Morality is spontaneous.

I remember hearing, early in my meditation practice, that meditators who had achieved a particular level of insight (understanding) would "no longer be able to break a precept (violate the *sila* code)." My experience is that I still make mistakes. I think I am aware of my errors sooner, and I make amends more quickly. I feel less guilt, perhaps more remorse, and as soon as I can make amends, I feel better. To avoid feeling demoralized, I remind myself, "Practice is called 'the Purification of the Heart,' and this is a sign that it's working."

At the end of my most recent visit to Jerusalem, in an interview with Rabbi Sheinberger in which I was thanking him for teaching me, I said: "And I also respect and admire you for never saying anything that might be *L'shon Hara* (bad speech)." The prohibition of *L'shon Hara* is the Jewish equivalent of the Buddhist practice of Right Speech.

I continued: "I've never heard you say any unkind thing about anyone. Even when people give you opportunities, even when people say something that encourages a critical remark."

Rabbi Sheinberger laughed. He said, "That's because I know that you put such a big emphasis on *L'shon Hara*—when you are here I never do it."

Torah All Around

THE TRUTH I KNOW IS THAT THE ESSENCE OF MIND
(Buddhists sometimes say mind/heart) is spacious clarity
and that the mind, unconfused, responds naturally with
friendliness, compassion, and generosity. And, I know that
identifying with the inevitable bouts of greed, anger, and
confusion that fill the mind in response to challenge is to
be enslaved. I also know that this truth is evident all the
time, in the middle of life as well as in special, set-aside
contemplative times, in every aspect of experience.

I read most Scripture as freedom or slavery stories. The
long story of the exodus from Egypt seems to me an ongoing reminder of the promise of freedom through steadfast
morality, triumph over greed and anger, and uncompromis-
ing faith rooted in understanding. Some stories seem self-
evident as freedom stories. Noah is easy. Noah didn't get
trapped into self-serving, ego-driven acts—indeed, he was
the *only* person on Earth who didn't, and he and his progeny
were granted life. I don't try to make the story plausible. I
read it as a cautionary tale. "Choosing life" means seeing
past the confusing thicket of personal impulses.

I was looking for another Torah example of renouncing
impulsive response in favor of considered response when
Shabbat Naso (Numbers, chapter 5) arrived. If I were choosing a date for my bat mitzvah, I would choose another
week. A central image of *Naso* is a jealous husband's indict-
ment of his wife's infidelity and her public humiliation. It
is unacceptable to my feminist sensitivities—what about

men's infidelities?—and I have a hard time reconciling humiliation with a religion I admire for its emphasis on respect for others. "How," I thought, "is Jonathan Slater [the rabbi at my synagogue] going to manage this?"

Jonathan managed it well. In his *d'var Torah* (Torah discussion) he said, "Why would the Torah, in a tradition that holds humiliation of another person as a dreadful act, describe public humiliation of a wife suspected of infidelity? It must be meant to show what terribly wrong choices a person might make acting reflexively from a mind filled with anger and jealousy. When we honor passing mind reactions as being *real*, worthy of responding to as guides for action," he continued, "we make them false gods."

After the service I said, "Jonathan, that was an amazing save of a virtually unacceptable, misogynist piece of Torah. I think you did a wonderful job, but really, you had to read it entirely as a trick, as a negative teaching that depended on its startle value to make its point."

"Well, that's a way you *can* read it," he said, "and rabbis do that."

Sometimes people ask me, "Why ally yourself with a Scripture that needs to be turned inside out in order to see the truth of it? Why not read a dharma that is more straightforward?" The answer is that for me the Torah is a very powerful symbol. It carries a strong, positive energy charge for me. So I am prepared to read Torah in any way that will make it meaningful, because I am *determined* to read it as a presentation of truth.

I realized that the Torah is a powerful symbol for me in the middle of a *dzogchen* (Tibetan Buddhist meditation) retreat some years ago. A Buddhist retreat seems perhaps an unlikely venue for that realization, especially because I was very happy practicing *dzogchen*, but it's true. In fact, my realization was related to how joyful I felt and even the *extra* delight I was experiencing *about* being joyful. My mind was peaceful, and I loved everyone.

Ordinary *dzogchen* practice is unremarkable looking. Normally retreats seem like mindfulness retreats. They are held in silence, and retreatants sit still or walk slowly, practicing alert presence. On the last day of practice, the lama leading the retreat conducted a Buddhist ritual ceremony, and since I like ritual, I was happy to attend. He chanted, raised and lowered a variety of ritual objects, rang bells. I was in a very good mood and anticipated—perhaps this is a sign of the never-ending nature of desire—feeling excited by the ritual. But I didn't. I became bored. At one point in the ritual, the lama raised a statue of Padmasambhava. Padmasambhava was not familiar to me but I recognized the swooping-up, holding-aloft gesture as the movement with which a Torah scroll is raised for the congregation to see after the Torah has been read. I thought, "I *wish* that were a Torah. Then I'd be feeling excited."

It was an important moment for me, but not because I think the goal of spiritual practice is to become excited. In fact, wanting *more* pleasure in the middle of feeling joy is more a sign of greed (and more work to be done) than it is of spiritual accomplishment. I did learn something, though, about the power of symbols and which symbols are powerful ones for me.

I talked to my friend Jack Engler about the images that arise in the mind during periods of deep concentration. I told him about the Scripture images that had been part of my meditation experience. Jack said that meditators predictably see images that reflect their particular religious tradition. He said, "They are spiritual icons."

I said, "*Icon* is not a word Jews are comfortable with."

And Jack said, "Yes, but remember that *icon* in Greek means *vehicle*, and vehicles take you places. If certain spiritual images bring delight and buoyancy to the mind and help it retain its natural clarity, they are skillful means."

My friend Helen Cohn is one of the rabbis at Temple Emanu-El in San Francisco, and we talked recently about "surrounding oneself with Torah." She described an experience she had just had with a group of twenty people at a Shabbat retreat. In order to let people see a whole Torah at one time, she had them unroll an entire scroll and stand in a circle holding it. A person in the middle, too far away to read the words, could still distinguish particular parts—the Ten Commandments are printed with unusually long blank spaces between them and *Parashat Haazinu*, at the end of Deuteronomy, is printed in two columns. Helen talked about people's experience of feeling "upheld" by Torah all around. We talked about the literal Torah being a close-up presentation of truth. Then we said that life itself, if we see it clearly, always provides the possibility of revelation. So that became the larger version of "Torah all around."

I've been thinking about that image since Helen and I talked about it. I've thought of the way in which I use Torah as the focusing lens for interpreting the world. If I use the central themes—freedom is possible, listen and pay attention, love your neighbor as yourself, and love God with all your heart—to keep my understanding balanced, I am more likely to respond to my life wisely. I think it works the other way, too. To whatever degree I am able to see the world wisely and keep truth clearly focused in my mind, I will see that truth in any story in the Torah.

Psalm 121

MY INTRODUCTION TO *DZOGCHEN* WAS AT A THREE-WEEK retreat at Lake Canandaigua, New York. I had no previous experience with Tibetan Buddhist practices, but I'd heard that the goal of *dzogchen* was the direct realization of the empty, insubstantial nature of phenomena. My previous experience with mindfulness practice had been realization through methodical practice over time. I was interested in direct realization.

I loved *dzogchen* practice. It was eyes-open practice, new for me, with gaze directed into space, looking at nothing. My discovery was that if I didn't look for something, if I looked at nothing, the same great spacious mind filled with joy and ease and peace that had been part of my mindfulness practice was my immediate experience. I was ecstatic. Literally.

Usually we practiced outdoors, and Lake Canandaigua is ringed by mountains. I sat on a bench near the lake, and, following instructions, lifted my gaze over the mountains. My sense of personal "I" dissolved, the urgency of my life's drama diminished, and I felt completely happy.

"Wait a minute!" I thought, jumping back into my separate memory bank of particular religious history. "There is a psalm that begins, 'I will lift up my eyes to the hills .... ' Which one *is* it?"

The Lake Canandaigua retreat center was a Catholic one, and the desk drawer in my room had a New Testament, but I was determined to find a Book of Psalms. "I'll bet that whole psalm is meditation instructions," I thought. "There must be a library here."

I walked through the retreat center, trying to look like a retreatant doing walking meditation, looking for a library. I passed an open door, saw a priest, clearly a resident of that monastery, sitting behind a desk. I glanced both ways, making sure I was alone in the hallway—after all, this was a silent retreat, and I am a retreat teacher who often urges people to "respect the silence." No one in sight in either direction. I stepped into the doorway of the office. The priest looked up. I said, "Father, which psalm begins, 'I will lift up my eyes to the hills?'"

He said, "It's 121. Do you want to see it?"

"Yes, I do," I replied.

"Here," he said, taking a Book of Psalms off his shelf. "Bring it back whenever you're finished with it."

I tucked the book under my jacket and walked, in what I hoped looked like contemplative mode, back to my room. I was, actually, quite flurried from my search adventure, my clandestine talking, and my eagerness to see if my "meditation instruction" intuition would prove to be true.

My English translation proved disappointing. "From whence . . . ?" sounded like a question, a question about the arrival of something. I had hoped for more. When I returned home, I phoned my friend Miles and said, "Is Psalm 121 a meditation instruction?"

He said, "What do you think it says?"

I replied, "I want it to mean that by looking out over the hills, by gazing at nothing, a direct realization of emptiness is possible and I think that's the ultimate help, the ultimate source of comfort."

"I think you can read it that way," Miles said. "After all, you could read *aleph, yod, nun* as *ayin*, 'nothing.' So you could translate the verse as 'I look up to the hills; my help comes from Nothing.'"

I don't think all of Psalm 121 is instructions. I think part of it may be read as reassurances and inspiration to practice. "Follow the instructions, and everything will be fine!"

A Jewish Translation of Psalm 121	A Buddhist Translation of Psalm 121
1. I lift up my eyes to the hills; where will my help come from?	1. Look at Nothing. Everything is revealed.
2. My help is from God, Who created heaven and earth.	2. Rest in the radiance of Natural Mind.
3. May God not permit your foot to waver, may your Guardian never slumber.	3. The joy of your discovery will strengthen your dedication to unwavering mindfulness.
4. The Guardian of Israel neither slumbers nor sleeps.	4. Because the perfection of emptiness, as the Source of creation, is always, always accessible.
5. God is your Guardian, God is the shelter at your right hand.	5. Whenever this is clear to you, wisdom and compassion will guide you.
6. The sun will not harm you by day nor the moon by night.	6. You will be safe.
7. God will guard you from all evil; God will protect your soul.	7. Your actions will be impeccable.
8. God will guard your going out and your homecoming from this time forth and for all the future.	8. Untroubled by fear and confusion, you will be peaceful and happy always.

Hineyni

HINEYNI, FOR ME, IS THE MOST POWERFUL WORD IN Genesis. Abraham says it to God. It means, "Here I am," but it is not a geographical answer. It is not the answer to "Where are you?" It is the response to the challenge to acknowledge the truth of the present moment, to recognize what needs to be done, and to be prepared to do it. Abraham says "*Hineyni*" three times in the most terrible of circumstances.

Mindfulness is also "Here I am, not hiding," and it is also an expression of freedom. Even when experience is painful, especially when it is dire, mindfulness is freedom from extra anguish, from the extra pain of futile struggle. "This is what is true. These are the possibilities. I understand the necessary response." And sometimes, "There are no possibilities other than surrender. So I surrender."

When I was a child and heard that some people were able to go to the gas chamber saying, "I believe with perfect faith . . . ", I didn't know what perfect faith was, but I knew that I wanted it. If it were possible, in such *unspeakable* situations, for speech—declarative, affirmative, fearless speech—to find its voice, I wanted to know "How?" I wanted to be able to do it.

I try to pray as if my prayers make a difference, but I don't believe that prayer saves us from terrible things happening. Terrible things do happen. I do believe that fully mindful prayer, undistracted presence, establishes the *capacity* of the mind to see clearly, and, when necessary, to surrender gracefully. *Hineyni*.

Hineyni is also the imperative to be fully present in moments of special joy, as well as in everyday moments of the amazing blessing of simply being alive. My father said grace at dinnertime, and sometimes, probably in an attempt to be modern and funny, he would say, "Well, here we are again, God."

That was it. The whole grace. Maybe that *is* the whole grace. Here we are. Here I am. *Hineyni.*

Serve God with Joy

I WAS SITTING ON A ROCK IN A FOREST IN NEW MEXICO in the middle of teaching a retreat and remembered a line in this manuscript—a line I'd written six months earlier— and I thought, "I think I was wrong. I need to change that." The line I remembered recounted an experience at a *dzogchen* retreat when I'd realized that the ritual ceremony would have been more exciting to me if it had used Jewish symbols. I'd added, "Of course, getting excited is not the point of spiritual practice." That was the only line I re- membered. I imagined I'd probably also said, "Insight and wisdom are what matters, excitement is impermanent, and being excited often clouds the mind . . . "—something like that, anyway. What I realized that morning is that being ex- cited is *crucial*. Perhaps *intoxication* with excitement might cloud the mind and allow for heedless behavior, but ex- cited states—zeal, enthusiasm, courage, vigor, curiosity— acknowledged and enjoyed within the context of serenity create buoyancy and interest in the mind. How else could we keep on going? *Why* else would we keep on going? The Buddha was certainly correct about all experience being in- substantial, void of anything providing sustaining satisfac- tion. But he also recognized the temporal presence of joy.

I remember teaching Buddhism, not very long after I'd begun studying it myself, to freshmen at Dominican College in San Rafael, California. I had begun—as I some- times still do—with the Four Noble Truths. Suffering seemed like unexpected bad news to these students. They were, for the most part, young people who had grown up in comfortable, caring families, who hadn't known a lot of struggle in their lives. They listened skeptically, glancing around to check their responses to what I was saying with one another. At one point someone said, "This religion seems *grim*." Someone else said, "Do Buddhists have birthday parties?" In fact, the Buddha taught a lot about joy, and although images of the Buddha don't look *jovial*, they do often portray him with a subtle smile. In addition to his title of "Buddha," which means "Awakened One," he was also called "The Happy One."

Not long ago I was sitting at Saturday morning services at my synagogue and not paying good attention. Usually I pay *serious* attention. I do it as a practice. But if I were describing my mind on that morning to meditation students, I would call it "mind full of thoughts" or "planning mind." Instead of resting in alert appreciation of present experience, my attention was captivated by a hypothetical future project.

The project that I continued to elaborate despite my periodic resolves to "Pay attention!" was the design of the *tallit* (prayer shawl) I would make for myself should I ever decide to wear one. Many of the women in my synagogue wear prayer shawls. I made prayer shawls—for Seymour, for my father, for my son Peter—twenty-five years ago when Peter was preparing for his bar mitzvah. I followed the instructions in the *First Jewish Catalog*. I hadn't previously considered one for me.

I have, however, definitely had *tallit* consciousness about my meditation shawl for many years. It stays folded on my *zafu* and when I wrap myself in it to sit, I quite consciously say, "Just as I wrap myself in this shawl now, so may my practice merit me in the future the clear mind of enlightenment." I have certainly enjoyed thinking how close this is to "Just as I wrap myself in this *tallit*, remembering as I do so my intention to fulfill all 613 of the *mitzvot* (commandments), so may I merit a beautiful *tallit* in the world to come." I just never thought about making a *tallit* for myself.

So when I found myself uncharacteristically inattentive to the Sabbath service and intrigued with prayer shawl designs, I wondered, "Why?" and "Why *now*?" I did more than wonder, though; I designed. I figured I would use my white woven meditation shawl that Seymour gave me as a gift years ago. It has done a lot of sitting with me. "I'd have to reinforce the corners," I thought, "and I remember how to tie *tzitzit* (fringes), but I don't recall how many windings. I'll have to look that up." The largest part of the fantasy was the design of the *atarah* (collar piece) that goes behind the neck and around the shoulders. "I could do it in needlepoint," I thought. "Maybe embroidery. It's more fluid. No, what I'll do is counted cross-stitch, and I'll use a fourteen-count white Aida cloth so I can do fine detail." All this while the bar mitzvah celebrant was chanting from Prophets and commenting on the text, and I could have just as well been on the moon for all I heard of it. "I'll have Liz design it on graph paper, and I'll do the cross-stitching. But I need the right words. What do I want?" This opened up the entirely new category of *p'sukim* (Scripture lines) that are meaningful to me. I alternatively chose and rejected. "Not quite right. Not *quite* right." The service was ending, and I'd missed most of it. I realized I had stood up and sat down and even sung prayers (at least I *think* I did) all with my attention somewhere else. I felt very light and cheerful about it. "I'll catch this *parashah* (Torah portion) next year," I thought. "Sometimes I'm present, sometimes I'm not. No big deal."

Seymour said, "What were you thinking about?"

I said, "If I ever make a *tallit* for myself, I'll stitch an *atarah* with *Ivdu Et Adonai B'Simcha* (Serve God with joy) on it."

"When did you decide that?" he asked.

"Just this second," I replied.

That evening I read from my book *It's Easier Than You Think* at a bookstore near my home. After the reading, someone came up and said, "I appreciated the advice you said you received from your teacher, 'Remember, be happy.' I understood what you meant about that being both an instruction *and* a wisdom teaching. When you say to a person, 'Remember, be happy,' you remind them that it is possible for the mind to be at ease whatever the circumstance. Just one more thing, though. I'm a Jew, and I'd like to know a way to say that Jewishly."

"Certainly," I said. "Serve God with joy."

Abounding Love

SOME MONTHS AGO A FRIEND REMARKED, "JUDAISM AS a religious path is limited because, at its very best, it develops a loving heart. It doesn't take the step of seeing through separateness to ultimate emptiness as the source of all form." I don't recall my exact response, but it doesn't matter because I have a more up-to-date response now. My current response also addresses a related remark I heard twenty years ago: "*Metta* (lovingkindness) practice is helpful as a concentration practice to steady the mind for insight practice, which is the only *true* path to enlightenment. With *metta* alone the practitioner is always trapped in the illusion that there is someone separate wishing well to someone else." I don't believe it. It's not my experience.

Recently, I was one of twenty people praying *Shacharit* (morning service) outdoors on the top of a hill, at Rose Mountain Retreat Center in New Mexico on the last day of a mindfulness retreat I was co-leading with my friend Rabbi Shefa Gold. We were chanting *Ahavah Rabah Ahavtanu* (With abounding love You have loved us), just those three words over and over. We stood in a circle, shoulders and arms touching, but not hands. That was important. I felt alone in my space, not *holding on*, but completely supported. I looked around at the people with me, now familiar to me because in my teaching role I'd met with each of them individually during the week and knew something of their stories. As always, because I have stylistic affinities and preferences, some of the people had seemed more on my wavelength than others.

I looked around at everyone in the circle and knew, happily, that I felt the same benevolence toward all of them. Plain benevolence. There aren't *degrees* of benevolence. Benevolence is impartial. A peaceful heart notices, and recognizes, and remembers, and *stays* peaceful. Once again, I discovered that a benevolent heart is the ultimate refuge and the ultimate support. Sylvia's memory was there, but Sylvia's ego-based flutterings of the heart toward and away from people weren't happening. "I am being God, loving abundantly," was my first thought. Then I realized, "No, God is loving these people abundantly through me because I'm not in the way. *I* am not here." My body and my perception and my memory were certainly operative but the sense of myself as separate—separate from any person or separate from God—had disappeared.

This is not a new discovery. I've known it for many years, unforgettably, since I put my foot down on a walking path in the middle of a mindfulness retreat in Yucca Valley, California, and knew for certain that no one was walking. What I enjoyed discovering (probably *re*discovering) is "This is how Jews discover emptiness!" And I thought about the chant we had done earlier, "God, the soul You gave me is pure," and thought, "I could say that as, 'The space through which consciousness appears to register on a personal level is absolutely boundless. All seemingly separating veils are illusions, shadows that block the light.'" I was having a good time. I thought about yesterday's chant, *Lev Tahor B'ra Li Elohim,* about which Shefa had said, "We could translate this as 'God created a pure heart for me' or 'Please, God, create a pure heart for me,' or even 'A pure heart creates God for me.'"

Afterward I said to her, "Shefa, I'm really excited about that third interpretation. It's the Buddhist *Brahmavihara* (Divine Abode) teaching: a completely spacious, unconfused mind rests in equanimity and radiates unrestrained *metta* (lovingkindness) and *karuna* (compassion). Translating those qualities back into Hebrew, we could say *chesed* (lovingkindness) and *rachamim* (compassion) and name them as divine qualities. Are you sure the grammar is right? Can we really interpret it as 'A pure heart creates God?'"

"Sure we can," she said. "It's *midrash* (interpretation). And we can take *midrashic* license."

Several weeks later Rabbi Arthur Green read this completed manuscript. He responded with his translation of *Lev Tahor B'ra Li Elohim:* "O Pure Heart! Make me a God!"

I recall reading an account many years ago, before I understood it, of a Catholic priest practicing Zen meditation in Japan. He had just told his teacher, "My attention becomes so focused that there is nothing left other than myself and God." His account continued, "And the abbot said, 'Pretty soon God will disappear,' and I said, 'Maybe *I* will disappear but God will never disappear,' and the abbot replied, 'It's the same thing.'"

I think the memory stayed with me twenty years as a riddle waiting to be fully understood because I shared the priest's reluctance to give up his attachment to God as conceivable and nameable. God language, however poetically nuanced, is a subtle place to hide attachment. Letting go of even that attachment—not by decision or intention, but by seeing clearly through it to the absolute emptiness of everything—is the birthplace of all possibility.

An Alternative, Almost Wordless, Liturgy

I HAVE A GROWING COLLECTION OF *SIDDURIM* (PRAYER books) because I love lingering over the poetry and the imagery, the differences in tone and style that characterize different religious perspectives. And part of my pleasure in belonging to a congregation that prays together is that we all always say the *same* words, aloud and in rhythm with one another. It is as regular and predictable as attending, calmly, to one breath after the next. Group prayer adds reassuring stability to my schedule. And it's also true that sometimes, in the middle of saying so many words, I long for more communal silent spaces.

I've imagined what it might be like to have silent services shaped by liturgical consciousness, perhaps informed by single words that orchestrate the consciousness work of liturgy with minimal sound. I was teaching with my friend Shefa, and I told her my fantasy.

"Maybe just three words," I said. "One word from Genesis—*Hineyni* (Here I am); one from the Passover Hagaddah—*Dayeynu* (It is enough for us); and one from Psalms—*Ashrey* (Happy)."

My idea was that people could sit together quietly, cultivating mindful presence. The group consciousness would be individual practice with the support that comes through feeling part of a group. The key word for that awareness of shared intent and commitment would be *Hineynu* (Here we are).

I imagined that *Dayeynu* (It is enough for us) might be the word people could think (or perhaps whisper) to acknowledge the peace of unconfused presence. Then I wondered, "How would I feel if someone whispered '*Dayeynu*' and *I* didn't feel peaceful? Would that demoralize me or inspire me? Perhaps," I said, "it would sustain me so that I could at least *sigh* '*Dayeynu*.' If I could *sincerely* say '*Dayeynu*,' whatever my situation, I would then be able to say '*Ashrey* . . . ' in appreciation of the natural contentment of the balanced mind."

Shefa and I mentioned our abbreviated liturgy discussion to the group, but since retreats are silent (except for instructions and liturgy), no one commented. The next day the whole group sat for a mindfulness practice period using the technique of focusing attention exclusively on hearing sounds. My experience with this practice is often the direct, intuitive understanding that my sense of personal self exists only in relationship. It is a most immediate way for me to remember that there is no *one* who is ever alone. My interconnectedness is *revealed* when I listen.

After the hearing meditation, Shefa said, "I think our liturgy must *also* contain the word *Sh'ma* (Hear!)."

Rabbi Judith HaLevy, one of the retreatants, exclaimed, "Finally! I've been waiting for two days for you to say that!"

Later we all added another word. "Amen."

Prayer

I PRAY. MY FATHER, A PERSON I MUCH LOVED AND
admired, said, "There's no such thing as a rational person
of faith" and so being prepared to pray seriously and then
being prepared to admit it has taken me a long time. My
prayer life is much younger than I am. It was born not long
after I was, but it didn't grow for long periods of time.
Internal promptings and external support have revived it.
But it is definitely a work in progress. I wonder if I should
be embarrassed ("You're sixty years old, Sylvia, you should
have figured this all out already") or pleased ("This is an exciting discovery time for me"). Actually I'm pleased. And
relieved. And grateful.

The God of my childhood was genderless but definitely
Other and approachable in prayer. My mother regularly
said, "God loves you." I liked the sound and the feel of my
mother saying, "God is taking care of you," even though I
secretly didn't believe I merited more attention than all the
other children in the world. I took God personally and comfortably. On Yom Kippur in the afternoon, if my headache
was really bad, I would eat something. My friend Eleanor,
much more disciplined than I, would watch me eat. I worried more about what Eleanor would think of me than what
God would think of me.

When I was fifteen years old, my mother had a stroke.
She, my father, and I had been sitting in our living room.
Suddenly, my mother couldn't speak, and her face seemed
contorted. My father said, "Phone Dr. G.," and I did, although my hands were shaking so it was hard to dial our

rotary telephone. An hour later, after the doctor had come, after the acute symptoms had passed and my mother could speak and was resting quietly, I went out onto our back porch and cried.

Dr. G. found me. Probably he meant to tell me that he was leaving. He stopped several feet away from me.

"That's not going to do any good," he said and turned and left.

He was wrong. It didn't heal my mother's stroke, and it didn't heal my pain, but it was the truest thing I felt. It was a *statement* of my pain and of my fervent prayer for my mother's life. Had words come to me in that moment, I would have said, "Please!" I wish Dr. G. could have said "Please" along with me. I'm sure he was thinking it.

MORE THAN TEN YEARS AGO, I was a participant at a mindfulness retreat on the island of Hawaii. One afternoon there was a tidal wave alert. We made emergency preparations. We moved crucial supplies, food and water, to the second story of one of the little bungalows in which we all lived and meditated. We sat quietly until the tidal wave alert time passed. As we were sitting, we heard the Catholics in our group celebrating Mass together in the next building.

I don't know how the Catholics found one another, but I thought about the fact that they did. There were lots of Jews there, but we didn't find one another or pray together. I think none of us knew that prayer can be the religious response to jeopardy as an expression of faith as well as a hope for rescue.

Joseph Goldstein, leading that retreat, told the story of the Zen master faced with imminent death from "the rising waters of the east and the west and the north and the south." When the Zen master was asked what he was going to do, he said, "I will just sit."

I think I remember the tidal wave story at this point for two reasons. One is the obvious one that it was a dramatic moment that serves as an example of the capacity of the mind to manage even very challenging situations gracefully. The other is that the experience of hearing Catholics praying together moved me, and retrospectively I mark it as one of the necessary but apparently not-yet-sufficient conditions to reactivate my own dedicated prayer life.

I learned about confidence from the story of the Zen master sitting and the sound of the Catholics praying. "Confidence isn't something we *have*," I thought, "it's something we practice." I decided the practice of steadfast confidence kept the mind balanced, "inclined the mind" to the insight that *everything* is manageable, absolutely everything. "I can stay present, and aware, for this experience" means "I believe with perfect faith . . ." Where a meditator might say, "I can still sit," a person with a prayer practice might say, "I can still pray." "Maybe," I thought, "at some point in practice, complete knowing becomes perfect faith."

MARC LIEBERMAN, A JEWISH Buddhist friend, asked me in an interview that was being videotaped, "If you have the capacity to use meditative techniques to create a mind state of spaciousness and ease, why complicate it with liturgy, with prayer?" He specifically cited the Kaddish prayer and said, "Do you think God needs praises?"

I don't recall what my answer was—probably it's on a piece of deleted videotape somewhere—but my recollection is that I offered some sort of response that justified the words. I probably said, "The very idea that God is beyond praises, unnamable—that cosmic design is beyond my personal comprehension—is a comforting one for me to remember." I might have said, "It's a formula for giving congregants an opportunity to praise God together." I might also have said, "It marks shifts between one level of liturgy and the next." Who *knows* what I said? After I finished, Laurel Criton, the filmmaker, said, "Very good textbook answer, Sylvia," meaning, I think, that I had sounded evasive. What I had been avoiding saying was, "I like prayers. I like the words. I don't know what I am praying *to*. Or if I am praying *to* anything. I just like praying."

I needed to be given permission as an adult to pray. My parents had tremendous Jewish pride and Jewish consciousness, but they didn't pray. My grandmother prayed. I learned prayers (and said them), but I was thirteen when my grandmother died and after that I didn't hear people talk about prayers as if they were real. Prayers assumed, I think, the status of the "Star-Spangled Banner"—something you sang with others to establish group membership. As a "sophisticated" college student, I was challenged by my friends—*and* by myself—about prayer with the question "To *whom* . . . ?" Not having a response, I stopped.

Rabbi Zalman Schachter-Shalomi gave me my first permission to pray. I met him in Berkeley in 1973. He was teaching a workshop on the *Tanya* (a classic Chasidic work) sponsored by the Aquarian Minyan. I fell in love with him immediately, but not because of what he said about the *Tanya*, which I didn't really understand. What excited me was the fact that he was a grown-up man, someone with scholarship and intellect that I admired, who talked seriously about God. What I found most compelling was the fact that he prayed, publicly, as if his relationship with God were real and intimate. I wanted that for myself. It took me another twenty years to admit it.

Miles Krassen was the person who taught me that prayer could be *practice*. I met Miles when we were invited to lead a class on prayer and meditation together at Elat Chayyim, the Jewish Renewal center in Woodstock, New York. The course was called "Mindfulness and *D'vekut*." *D'vekut* is the Hebrew word for cleaving, and it describes a particular meditation style. Although Miles and I had never met before, teaching together was a magical experience. We discovered that we were speaking as if with one voice. All the questions of "Are you a Jew?" and "Are you a Buddhist?" were clearly irrelevant. They were names of forms, shortcuts for identification. The question for both of us was "What is your spiritual goal?" and on that level, we understood each other perfectly.

At the end of our week of teaching together Miles said to me, "I love you. I think you are a wonderful teacher. And you taught better whenever you let your *Yiddishkeit* (Jewishness) show. And I think you would do well with a regular prayer practice. You could start with *Minchah* (afternoon prayers) because that's the shortest. And memorize the *Amidah* (special prayer recited during all three daily prayer services that contains nineteen separate blessings and petitions), so that while you say it you can keep your eyes closed and focus your attention in these energy centers (*sefirot*), which I'm drawing for you right now. And, in addition, try going outdoors by yourself and find a place where you feel secluded and talk to God. Just talk." He gave the instructions separately—not all at one time—but I remember them as my initiation to formal prayer practice *and* permission.

It was permission to do what I had been wanting to do but had felt foolish about doing. I needed a grown-up person, one that I admired, to say, "Do it." It probably also counts that Miles said, "I love you."

I THINK OF THE PASSIONATE responses of my heart as an ongoing, spontaneous prayer, and I recognize my moment-to-moment attempts to stay alert and balanced as my natural response to finding myself in a life, in a world, in a universe far beyond my control or comprehension. As a Buddhist, I name this re-collecting of myself mindfulness. As a Jew, I think of it as *t'shuvah* (return).

Liturgy as discipline often seems to me like spoken or chanted mindfulness. It mandates presence. It offers formulas for acknowledging both joy and pain. Sometimes I feel my prayers are practice—like mindfulness practice—to help compose my mind, refocus on the moment, and possibly "incline my mind to insight." *Inclining the mind* is a term I learned from one of my Buddhist teachers. It means "calling to mind something that you intellectually know is true in order to be able to understand it more directly, more completely." Sometimes the content of a specific prayer, one that I've said many times before, catches my attention and seems especially significant. Suddenly the words illuminate something new for me—something about how *I* am (a personal insight), or something about how *things* are (a religious insight). At both times I wonder, "Why didn't I see that before?"

Most often I don't have the sense of praying *to* anything. I'm just praying. "This is what I'm happy about." "This is what I'm unhappy about." "This is what I'm hoping for." "This is the consciousness I'd like to have with me now—alert, focused, accepting, noncombative—and these prayers help me stay in touch with my experience and my intention." I'm not actually saying these particular words; I'm saying prayers—generally traditional ones—and they are a familiar shorthand. Prayers make me feel good. I love them.

The truth of my liturgy practice is that I began with Miles's suggestion of *Minchah* and found over time that morning prayers suited me more. In the morning I can sit for a while before I begin with formal liturgy. Sometimes I study for a while. Then I sit. Then I pray. A part of my liturgy practice that is pleasing to me is my commitment to do *some* formal practice every day. What I do changes from day to day.

Most often when I am alone, I sit quietly until formal liturgy begins by itself. Words arise in me in response to my feeling present and centered that are variations of praise and thanksgiving for feeling sheltered in the protection of spacious mind. It makes sense to me that traditional communal morning worship begins *"Mah Tovu Ohalecha"* (How good your tents are!) as a recognition of safety. My prayers often start farther along in the liturgy, sometimes with a list of blessings (gratitude for my life), sometimes with *Ahavah Rabah Ahavtanu* (With abounding love You have loved us). This means that I am actually beginning in the middle of the liturgy—*Ahavah Rabah* comes right before the *Sh'ma*—but liturgical correctness becomes eclipsed by devotional honesty. When I feel present and focused and alert, I quite literally feel warm and held. I feel, "With a great love You love *me* . . . "

Often when I pray alone, I don't use a prayer book. I like to concentrate on what I'm saying, and I do that better with my eyes closed. I have been memorizing more and more of the liturgy. I'm a good memorizer, so that's not a chore for me. Also, I like reading prayer books in order to memorize. I like looking at the words intently; I like considering the variations of translations different commentators offer; I like looking at the way the same words appear in different print styles.

I try to bring the same diligent attention to mindfulness practice and to liturgy. If I look for nuances of difference in my experience, I can find them. When I am mindful, things just *are.* The sense of an observer and experience being observed changes to a sense of just experience happening. When I pray, my sense of myself— Sylvia with a story— does not disappear. I think words always create a sense of separateness. Both in prayer and in meditation I feel a sense of intimacy. I feel loved and supported and fearless.

When I sit with a group, the silence feels companionable. When I pray with a group, prayer seems companionable. And I am young enough in my prayer life, and still excited enough by it, to have what Suzuki Roshi, the founder of the San Francisco Zen Center, called "beginner's mind." Suzuki advised his students to guard against practice becoming routine and encouraged them to bring the same hopeful anticipation that accompanied their first meditation to every subsequent one. I assume I will learn something from the style of every *minyan* (prayer group) I pray with. My regular weekday *minyan* reads Hebrew faster than I read English. I asked my friend Helen, "Are they really reading every word?" She said, "I don't think so. I think they just look at the page and recognize the meaning because they've said it so often." I tried it. Psalm 148. Psalm 149. Psalm 150. Speed psalming. I now know what's in each of them, so I've stopped trying to read every word. I read the first two lines, I look at the whole page, and I read the last two lines. I've discovered it's a good style for intensifying concentration. And anyway, we *do* sing Psalm 150.

When I pray with my group, I finish the liturgy. When I pray by myself, especially if I've been sitting for a while in silence, particular words or phrases become so inspiring, so fascinating, that I get lost (maybe the more proper word is *found*) in them for long stretches of musing time. This is the place at which for me a distinctly defining difference between meditation and prayer disappears.

I recently spent all of the time I had set aside for prayer meditating on the phrase "Love your neighbor as yourself." A friend of mine had written me a letter mentioning that Rabbi Isaac Luria, a sixteenth-century Kabbalist, taught that dedicating ourselves to the intention to love others as ourselves is the prerequisite for prayer. Although I had heard the commandment many times before, on that particular morning I *understood* it more clearly than ever. (In Buddhist terms, this would be an *insight*, something a person knew before and now knows profoundly.)

I began to muse about how I would teach "Love your neighbor as yourself" as a Buddhist. I might say, "We think in terms of separations: 'myself,' 'my neighbor'— 'mine,' 'his,' and 'hers.' Because seeing and hearing and thinking and feeling all happen, we imagine that some*one* is inside us, an actor in a story with a history and a future. And, we imagine other actors, the owners of other bodies and other stories. We develop particular affinities and enmities. When we see through the illusion of separateness, we understand that we share joys and sorrows with all other human beings. We realize the shared, universal truth of suffering and however much people appear as neighbor, everyone becomes family, as dear as kin, as dear as ourselves."

AT THE END OF ONE OF MY VISITS to Jerusalem, I said to Rabbi Sheinberger, "I'd like to have a homework for this year, please. I'd like to do a meditation on a prayer."

He said, "All right. What prayer do you want?"

I was a bit surprised. I had thought he would *assign* me one, based on some intuitive sense of what he thought I needed. (I begin to see how I portray myself—to myself and to others—as the plainest of nonsentimental nonromantics, while secretly always hoping for mystery.)

"I'd like *Ahavah Rabah Ahavtanu*," I said. "It appeals to me. I think it mentions everything important. If I had only thirty seconds for liturgy, that's what I'd say."

"Okay," Rabbi Sheinberger said, "Come back tomorrow, and I'll give you a meditation on *Ahavah Rabah*."

The next day we sat at our usual places at his long table. Rabbi Sheinberger at one end, Seymour to his right, I at the other end of the table. Rabbi Sheinberger began a long discourse about the talmudic debate over whether the first words of the prayer should be *Ahavah Rabah* (great love) or *Ahavat Olam* (eternal love). He ended by saying that since no conclusion had been reached, people traditionally say "*Ahavah rabah*" at *Shacharit* (morning services) and

"Ahavat olam" at *Minchah* and *Ma'ariv* (afternoon and evening services).

"Oh dear," I was thinking. "Is this his idea of meditating on a prayer? I've told him I want a prayer homework to work on all year, and I hoped to be able to come back next year and say something to him about my homework experience. I can't do this kind of talmudic debate study. My Hebrew isn't good enough yet!"

"Now, here is your homework," Rabbi Sheinberger said. He took out a piece of loose-leaf paper on which he had written the *Ahavah Rabah* prayer. Instead of writing it out as a paragraph, he had written it down the right-hand margin of the page—a list of phrases, some individual words, some short sentences.

"What should I do with this?" I asked.

"Just look at it," he said. "Every day, when you say it, say it slowly, and look at each word. See what it tells you."

I felt inspired and enthusiastic. Now the homework sounded like what I imagined prayer-meditation would be. I'd recently read somewhere, "There are some people who can only pray with a pen in their hand," and I'd thought, "That sounds like me." Sitting and reflecting, and musing and intuiting, and writing it all down at the end—and doing it all about a prayer I loved—was *exactly* the right homework for me.

A year later, I gave my homework report: "I did what you said. I looked at the words carefully. Usually the meaning of the words didn't change but their importance changed. Sometimes a word or even a whole sentence became very important. It was as if the letters got larger on the page. When that happened, I thought about those words for a while."

He said, "Good."

I said, "One line, though, always has a particular meaning to me. When I say *"Vehaviyeynu l'shalom meyarbah kanfot ha'aretz"* (And bring us in peace from the four corners of the earth), I don't think about *people*. I think about attention. When my attention is distracted and my mind is confused, I don't feel 'at peace.' So, when I say that line, I am trying to collect scattered attention."

Rabbi Sheinberger considered a moment. Then he said, "That sounds good, too."

I THINK A LOT ABOUT the instruction in *The Way of the Pilgrim:* "Pray without ceasing." I felt I was praying without ceasing when I did intensive *metta* (lovingkindness) practice. What I'd really like is for my life to be a prayer, an offering of thanksgiving. I could do it if I were always present, but I'm not. I'd even be happy with *usually* present. I'd like to be clear enough, often enough, to not get hopelessly tangled up in confusing, ego-centered demands. I'd like to remember that I am happiest when I feel loving. I used to say to myself, as my combination confidence-talk and *kavannah* (intention statement), each time I sat on my meditation cushion, "May I be able to stay present for whatever comes up next." Later I realized I was using it off the cushion as well. I don't need to ask to be *able* to love. I only need to hope to be present. When I am present, loving happens by itself.

I discovered, with great delight, that the nineteenth benediction of the *Amidah* scans exactly into the melody I use for singing *metta* resolves. I use the afternoon or evening versions, because the morning version—a few phrases longer—doesn't fit. The intent of *Shalom Rav* (Great peace) is the same as *metta* intent: "May all beings be peaceful."

Since my habit, from *metta* practice, is continuous resolves, I feel quite prepared to sing *Shalom Rav Metta* apart from formal prayers. I once spent a week doing hermitage retreat practice at Redwoods Monastery in Whitethorn, California. I spent hours every day in their garden, weeding and singing just that one benediction, over and over, to myself.

"Far out!" I thought. "I'm in a Trappist Monastery singing *Shalom Rav* to my *metta* melody. And I'm happy."

WHEN PEOPLE TALK TO ME about prayer, they often ask, "Do you think prayer works?" and what they mean is, "Do you think your prayers affect the *outcome* of a particular situation?" That question suggests that the trustworthiness of prayer seems to depend on results. I hold that question differently. Sometimes the most fervent prayers seem unanswered. Other times miracles seem to happen. It's a mystery to me. A prayerful life seems to me the universal response to that mystery.

Buddhists pray, just as Jews do, for the healing of people who are sick and for the safe passage of people who have recently died. Jan Bays, a Zen teacher, led the morning meditation at a recent gathering of Buddhist teachers of all three lineages. After an hour of silent sitting, we all chanted, in English, part of a Zen *sutra* (Scripture) on compassion. At the end of the communal chant, Jan continued, in chant rhythm, to intone "and we ask special blessings for those people who have recently died and we name . . . "

(and she mentioned names and everyone in the group mentioned names). Then she continued, "And we think particularly of those people now struggling with illness such as . . . " (and she named names and all of us offered names). Asking for blessings was part of the Dedication of Merit closure of our meditation session, "May our practice be on behalf of all beings and especially these beings." Asking for blessings is a part of Buddhist prayer life just as it is a part of Jewish prayer life. It seems natural.

I am reluctant to admit, "Sometimes I plead with God," because I hear the echo of my father's voice saying, "There is no such thing as a rational person of faith," and I don't want to appear irrational. I don't often plead. The petitions that are part of my daily prayer life feel like intentions rather than asking for special favors. I usually feel fine about saying "Y'hi ratzon" (May it be Your will). I understand those words as "Karma is true," "The cosmos is correct," and "Everything is unfolding perfectly." I feel comforted rather than dismayed by my own insignificance.

On the other hand, when I am frightened, I pray unashamedly as if God cares about *me*. If my child is having a diagnostic CAT scan, or my grandchild is being delivered by emergency cesarean section, I am not saying "Y'hi ratzon." I am saying "Please! Please!" And if there is enough time, I phone people I know to ask them to say "Please!" with me. I don't do it because I *know* prayers are answered or understand how prayers are answered. My prayers, when people I love are in jeopardy, do not arise from a place of rational choice. In my heart of hearts, I know and I accept that it is all Y'hi ratzon, but I pray "Please" because it is all I can do and it sustains me.

There is one more thing I need to say about my prayer life. It comes last because I am still shy about it. I am only recently becoming able to articulate it clearly, and I am certain that it would not have been revealed to me without my mindfulness practice, which caused me to fall in love with life—*all* of life. Although loving appears chronologically as the most recently emerging aspect of my prayer life, I am guessing it has always been its foundation.

These past few years I've explained my prayer life—to friends, colleagues, teachers, students—sensibly: prayer as practice, prayer as discipline, prayer as mindfulness, prayer as the source of insight and revelation. I've hinted at the truth when I've said, "I remember my mother's voice saying, 'God loves you, Sylvia.'" I've gotten closer to telling the truth when I've said, "I love prayers." I have not, until now, been ready to say, "I love God."

"Wait a minute!" I can hear my father's voice, along with many other voices: "Didn't you say your God was formless, beyond naming, beyond description?"

"Yes, of course I did. But not beyond loving."

I was having lunch with a friend, one of my prayer confidants, and he said, "How much of your prayer practice is devotional, Sylvia?"

I said, "Well, you know, I'm not really a *bhakti* [Hindu word meaning devotional type]. Besides, liturgy is more respectful than romantic—'Your servant' more than 'Your lover.'"

"Look outside of liturgy then," he said. "Find something else. Read *Shir HaShirim* (Song of Songs)."

"I don't know . . . "

"Just try it for a week," he said. "Even the first line,

'*Yishakayni Min'shikot pihu*' (May He kiss me with the kisses of his mouth . . .). Say it over and over. See what happens."

I left our lunch feeling the eager, aroused excitement that is the response to someone saying, "I'm about to introduce you to someone I know you'll love."

"Should I use that *pasuk* (Scripture line)," I wondered, "or should I choose another?" I thought of other phrases that were expressions of love. At one point on my drive home, I noticed my hands on the steering wheel. The ring on my right hand is one that Seymour gave me twenty years ago. It says, *Ani L'Dodi V'Dodi Li* (I am my beloved and my beloved is mine.)

I began to think about the word *Dodi*. It means "my beloved." I think of it as "my dearest friend, my closest intimate." Seymour and I use "*Ani L'Dodi V'Dodi Li*" to sign letters to each other.

When I arrived home I read Song of Songs. The second phrase of the first line is "*Ki Tovim Dodeycha Miyayin*" (Your loving is better than wine). I decided that was my phrase. Because I usually sing my prayers, I looked for a melody that worked for those words. My *metta* tune is perfect. By and by I added *Yishakeyni*. The same tune accommodates all of it.

A week later I had lunch with my friend again. "Okay," I said, "I'm a *bhakti* . . . "

I AM, THESE DAYS, HAPPILY overcoming my shyness and am grateful for my friends who talk about prayer with me. Just recently I met Judith HaLevy, a rabbi in Los Angeles, at a silent meditation retreat in New Mexico. During the three-hour drive together from the retreat center to the Albuquerque Airport at the end of the retreat, we talked continuously with the open trust of lifelong friends. "What is your practice?" "What are your concerns?" "What are you studying?" "Whom are you learning with?" And finally, "How do you pray?"

I was already in line for my boarding pass, with Judith still with me since her flight had not yet arrived, when I made my final disclosure. "This last year," I said, "my prayers have become more *bhakti*. It's been wonderful."

Judith asked, "What are you using as prayers?"

I told her some of my favorites.

She said, "Try *Yedid Nefesh* (Beloved of my soul). It's marvelous."

After Judith left I realized I was in an airport boarding lounge full of people who had all disappeared in the intensity of the prayer conversation. I felt happy to see them. I explained, in Spanish, to the woman standing next to me that the number 139 on her boarding card meant that she needed to wait, with me, to board the airplane after everyone else. She said, "*Gracias.*"

I thought, "It's *all* grace." Then I thought, "The ultimate prayer, the prayer that comes from deepest wisdom, is 'Thank-you!'"

Liturgical Optimism

SOME OF MY BUDDHIST FRIENDS, ESPECIALLY THOSE who grew up as Jews, ask, "How do you deal with a male God? Do you really pray to God as King? Do you pray to the easily-annoyed God of the Bible?" I've been needing to work on answers that speak to the concerns *behind* people's questions. My truest response is "I read through those parts; they don't fit my experience."

"How *can* you read through those parts?" and "*Should* you read over them?" would be good rebuttals to my perhaps too facile answer.

I think that I am not indifferent to the pain women and men have experienced in nonegalitarian situations, but patriarchal prayer language doesn't push any buttons for me. I don't have a history of personal pain around patriarchy. My father loved and admired my mother, who was independent and intellectual, and he happily took on an extra job teaching night school to pay for my college tuition.

Also, I never thought of God as having a body or a gender. The gender-God statements that begin or end prayers and blessings feel to me like ritual formulas for getting into and out of the text of the prayer—the heart-alignment-intention part of prayers—the part most meaningful to me.

I sometimes remember, when I make blessings with my grandchildren, to say "*Nevareych et eyn hachaim . . .* " (Let us bless the Source of Life) in place of "Blessed are You Lord our God, King . . . ", but I often forget. In any case, their school and their family are still saying "King." I don't mind using "King" with children. The idea of "King"—a great power in charge who takes care of everyone—is one that I think resonates more with children than "Source." "Sources" don't take care of you. Moms and dads and kings and queens do. "King of the Universe" and "Sabbath Queen" are acceptable to me for childhood religious consciousness. I think as an individual's understanding shifts from "person" and "other" to "source" and "connection," gender-words can be replaced by subtle concept words. Or they can be the shorthand for subtle concept words.

A few years ago I was an invited speaker at a Jewish women's retreat in Mendocino, California. It was one of the first times I was asked to teach Buddhist meditation specifically to Jews, and I was excited about it. The drive to Mendocino took longer than I had anticipated, and I arrived just as the Opening Circle Ritual was about to begin. Margaret Holub, the rabbi who had invited me, greeted me warmly. "We were just about to begin," she said. "Why don't you light these candles as the opening of our retreat? You could light them as if this were a holiday." I felt honored. I said something about intention, something else about my delight in being there, and I lit the candles and said the blessing for lighting holiday candles. As soon as I said it, I realized that I had, in my excitement, lapsed into my private patriarchal prayer form. Nobody mentioned it. I didn't think anyone would, but I did think they all heard it. "Probably," I thought, "they just think I am old."

When my friend Rabbi Sheila Weinberg read this manuscript, she said, "You need to say more about this, Sylvia. Gender liturgy is an important issue. Many women have been hurt by the patriarchy of the Judaism they grew up with."

I didn't know what else I could say until I watched my grandson Collin praying with his second-grade class at

Brandeis Hebrew Day School. On those Fridays when his class is in charge of running the Shabbat services, Seymour and I are among the other parents and grandparents sitting in the back of the Congregation Rodef Sholom feeling proud and pleased. What particularly pleases me is seeing girls and boys equally at ease presiding at a prayer service.

Second-graders are small, only eight years old, so they require the help of their teacher to remove the Torah from its special cabinet. Once the Torah is placed on the reading table, the students themselves unroll it, find their place in it, and begin one by one to read the weekly Torah portion. As I watched two eight-year-old girls unroll a Torah, scan up and down the columns to find the right place to start, and begin reading, completely unselfconsciously, I thought, "They have no *idea* that this used to be a problem. They have no sense that there's anything unusual about women touching or handling or reading from the Torah." I felt all right about them saying "King" because they all had equal access to the Torah. I have not yet told Collin that I never touched a Torah until four years ago when Sheila handed one to me in the middle of a Shabbat service at the Barre Center for Buddhist Studies.

I rejoice at the accessibility of Torah wisdom. Probably over time, as communities find it useful, liturgy will also change. It always has. My contribution to its changing is my intention, when making blessings with my grandchildren, to remember to say, "*Nevareych . . .* "

Serve God with Sorrow

MANY YEARS AGO, NOT LONG AFTER I HAD BEGUN MY
meditation practice, I overheard a conversation between two
of my teachers as I was folding towels in the corner of the
staff dining room. One of them said, "I'm hoping my practice will allow me a deeper understanding of suffering."

I thought to myself, "Oh God, I have all I can do manag-
ing the suffering I feel. I don't want anything deeper."

It's twenty years later now and my perspective has
changed. I think—actually I know—that my response came
from fearful preoccupation with the possibility of the loss
of the people I love most. I was so frightened by my awareness of the inherent fragility of life that I couldn't think
clearly. What I've learned in twenty years is that everything
is manageable. I'm not hoping for deeper painful challenges, but I know that the ones I've had have made me
kinder and more compassionate. When I can't hide, or
don't hide, from the pain in my life or in lives around me, I
am heartbroken. And I'm convinced that compassion depends on clear-minded understanding of suffering. When I
am heartbroken, if I am not *frightened*, I am able to serve.

My friend Helen is a rabbi, and she and I talked recently
about the difference between equanimity and indifference.
Helen had just officiated at a funeral. She said, " I usually
feel sad about deaths, sometimes very sad. Other times I
wonder if I feel sad *enough*. I wonder if my response is genuine wisdom or just numbness from too many funerals."
We told each other stories we knew as examples of dealing
with grief.

First we told Jewish stories. Helen mentioned the Talmud account of B'ruryah, the wife of Rabbi Akiva's disciple Rabbi Meir, who broke the news of the death of their two sons to her husband by saying, "What if someone gave you two jewels for safekeeping and then came to reclaim them?" We wondered if her response was an act of faith, the acceptance of *dayan emet* (God is the true judge).

I told the story of the Piazetzner Rebbe who learned of the death of his hospitalized son just before nightfall on Friday, celebrated Shabbat with normal prayer and teaching, told his wife the news after *havdalah* (end-of-Sabbath ritual) on Saturday night, and then cried. We talked about the *halachah* (Jewish law) that precludes mourning on Shabbat. "Did the Piazetzner Rebbe actually feel grief-stricken?" we asked each other, or "Did his awareness of God, through Shabbat consciousness, erase his sadness?"

Then we told Buddhist stories. I said, "I know a Zen story about an abbot, threatened by a samurai who said, 'I could run you through with my sword without blinking an eye.' The abbot's response was, 'I could be run through with a sword without blinking an eye.' Do you think," I said, "that the abbot was so clear about the truth of suffering that he was unattached to life?"

"On the other hand," Helen said, "I heard you tell about a Zen master who cried when his son died."

I said, "He did. His students said, 'Didn't you tell us that death is normal and inevitable? That everything is impermanent?' The Zen master said, 'It is, and I'm still sad.'"

"Wait a minute," I said, "Let's figure out what these stories mean. They can't be prescriptions about how people should act because everyone responded differently."

"No one was frightened," Helen said. "Everyone stayed present."

I said, "I think that's it. I think fearlessness inspires. Even *relative* fearlessness. I taught a meditation seminar in Los Angeles the year my son Peter had cancer. My whole family was worried and sad and so was I. I didn't tell my students my story, but when I taught the Noble Truth about attachments causing suffering, I said that I still had attachments and I still suffered."

"What happened?" Helen asked.

"They all sat there," I replied, "looking stunned. I asked, 'Does anyone have questions?' No one did. I thought, 'Oh God, I have totally blown this whole seminar. I've announced that I'm not enlightened. I have two days to go, and I have already lost everyone's confidence.' I continued with sitting instructions, walking instructions, Dharma talks—everybody practiced but no one spoke. At the end of the day when the retreat silence was over, someone said, 'You seemed subdued, so I know you have troubles. But it inspired me that you were here and that you taught.' Someone else said, 'From the beginning, when you said you still suffered, I knew you were telling the truth. And then I knew I could trust you.'"

"What were they trusting?" Helen asked. "That you were honest? That you weren't frightened? *Weren't* you frightened?"

"Sometimes I was," I said. "When I thought about possible future scenarios, When I thought 'What *if* . . . ?' When I stayed present, I wasn't frightened. Just sad. Then I was okay. I think that's what they trusted."

Holocaust

I AM SURE THAT THE ESSENCE OF CLEAR MIND IS impartial lovingkindness and unwavering compassion. My experiences of intensive practice have included instances of being so bowled over by a rush of loving feeling for a person walking down the hall toward me—even a person I didn't know at all—that I've needed to lean against the wall to keep from falling over. At those times, a bird chirp has become the most incredibly gorgeous sound I've ever heard, and I've thought, "Now I know the meaning of the word 'swoon'!" I have felt exalted about being human, about sharing with other humans the fundamental capacity for limitless loving as well as the response the texts name as the "quivering of the heart" in compassion.

I know that I act unskillfully when I am confused by greed, hatred, and delusion. I know these are the roots of evil. I am saddened by the magnitude of cruelty in the world. Sometimes I am frightened. When I am confused by fear, there is no possibility for clear seeing, and I lose heart. At those times, I don't remember that compassion is the redemptive response to suffering.

Several of my friends told me, "You can't write a book about being a Jew, Sylvia, without talking about the Holocaust." I insisted that I could. I said, "I don't think it's relevant to this book. I'm describing how my meditation practice and Dharma understanding have made me more awakened as a Jew."

"That makes it even more important," my friends said. "It's not possible to be a Jew and not be affected by the Holocaust. It's not possible to be a person of faith and not have some response." They were right.

I was nine years old when the war in Europe ended and relatives of my father who had survived began to arrive in New York. They would live with my family briefly and then move on. I listened to grown-up conversations from the edge of the living room. My mother told me, when I asked her, that cousin Baile's ankles were so swollen because she had lived outdoors in a Polish forest for two years and her feet had been frostbitten. Baile's brother Yoshe told stories about smuggling goods across a border to earn some money, and people smiled at his cleverness. Baile's husband, Moshe, had been a veterinarian before the war, and all three of them moved to New Jersey and began a chicken farm together. Ten years later Seymour and I spent part of our honeymoon at their farm, hand-sorting eggs as they rolled down a conveyer belt, sleeping at night in an enormous cloud of a European featherbed.

Cousin Aaron had also been a veterinarian in Europe. He had been given refuge in the hayloft of a neighbor's barn throughout the war. He said that German troops searched the barn periodically, randomly piercing with pitchforks the hay under which he was hidden. I remember him saying that he had only one book with him for the three years that he spent in the barn—an American history text. Cousin Aaron moved to Chicago and married, and his children were born before Seymour and I married. When our son Michael was born, the Chicago cousins regularly sent boxes of outgrown baby clothes as gifts for us. The boxes from Chicago had special significance to me. I always remembered the hayloft.

The Canadian cousins couldn't get entry visas into the United States and so could stay with us only briefly before moving on to Canada. I remember them preparing for the long train journey, first north into Canada and then across Canada to Saskatoon. They worried about not being able to speak English. My parents coached them. Over and over they practiced: "I am sorry. I dunt hunderstent you. Pleece hexcuse me." One of them gave me a child's gold ring etched with black filigree with one tiny diamond in it. I wore it for many years. Much later, after I discovered I'd lost the ring, I realized it must have belonged to a child who died.

In summer camp during those years we sang, in Yiddish, "Never say that you are walking the last road . . . ," the resistance song of the Warsaw Ghetto. The last lines are, "This is a song of people trapped inside crumbling walls, a song sung with guns in the hands." We also sang, "I believe with perfect faith in the coming of the Messiah. And even if His coming is delayed, I will continue to believe."

I was forty-four years old when I visited a German-speaking country for the first time. Seymour and I booked a cruise on the Danube from the Black Sea to Vienna on a Romanian tour boat. The boat was small, serviceable but definitely not luxurious, and we were the only English-speaking passengers. Most of the others were Germans, coworkers in a factory on a company-sponsored holiday. I sat on the deck reading a paperback book whose subtitle was "How could a civilization that produced a Goethe and a

Schiller also produce a Hitler?", which I had covered in a brown paper wrapper in order not to offend.

At night after dinner, a trio—two accordions and a baritone horn—played in the tiny salon adjacent to the dining room. The Germans invited us to join them and shared their wine with us. I spoke my most careful college German, quite sure that my Yiddish accent would be evident to all of them. One evening, a man named Fritz asked me to waltz with him and I did. We struggled through conversation with my stilted German until, at some moment, we discovered that we both spoke French. We laughed. Talking and dancing became easier.

"Where did you learn to speak French?" I asked and, as I did so, I realized I already knew the answer. He was, I judged, several years older than I was. I had just that afternoon read a description of the last days of the war in France, something like, "By that time the Germans had virtually run out of material and were reduced to fighting with manpower only. They used teenage conscripts." The sentence I still remember was "The fields of northern France were covered with the bodies of seventeen-year-old German boys."

I looked at Fritz. A pink-cheeked man, a company worker traveling with his wife, a man with three sons at home, who shared his wine with me and asked me to dance knowing that my German was Yiddish accented. He hesitated a moment.

"I was stationed in France with the troops during the war," he said.

"I guessed that," I answered.

We finished the dance and had some more wine.

The next day another German in Fritz's group sat down near me on the deck. "I have a Jewish friend," he said. I smiled at him. I had felt a shift in myself the night before in the moment when it dawned on me that Fritz must have been in France, because I had realized at the same moment how glad I was that *he* wasn't dead. I felt that my deck companion was making the "friend disclosure" to let me know about his pain.

In 1992, Seymour and I were bicycling in Austria, and someone said, "You ought to see Berlin now that the wall is down." In Berlin someone said, "There is a wonderful chain of lakes north of here. You can rent a houseboat for several days." The boat rental office in Furstenberg is on the shore of a large lake. The rental agent said, "Your boat won't be ready until tonight. Why don't you ride your bikes around the lake? There's a lot to see. Look across behind you. That's Ravensbrook. Many people go there." The lake is wide and the only thing I could discern clearly was the smokestack chimney.

The sign outside Ravensbrook says that it was the only camp exclusively for women and children and that 350,000 of them died there. I said to Seymour, "Don't stand near me and don't walk near me. If we go in, the only way I can possibly hold this is in silence. One word and I won't be able to bear it."

We took a long time going through and stayed away from each other. One former cell block has individual rooms dedicated to women and children of particular countries. The Romanian room. The Czechoslovakian room. Designs of artists from each different country saying silently what cannot possibly be said. In the hallways there are glass museum cases with bits of embroidery, children's copybooks, baby shoes. Finally, the crematorium and the oven whose smokestack we saw from across the lake.

When we met afterward outside to get on our bikes and pedal back around the lake, we couldn't look at each other. "No talking now either," we agreed.

The next morning was sunny. Seymour was signing the houseboat rental papers in the sales office. I was standing at the counter in the kitchen of our boat making sandwiches. I looked out the window and saw two men in Russian Army uniforms stroll by. The Russians had been the invading, occupying troops here for fifty years, but they were scheduled to leave at the end of the summer and everyone was relaxed. A very large ferry that had been docked near our berth blew its whistle to let last-minute shore-stragglers know the boat was about to leave. I looked across onto the deck and watched people waving at friends on shore. A summer party scene. An oompah band started up as the ferry pulled away from its berth. They played "Anchors Aweigh." I didn't turn around to watch the ferry leave because I knew Ravensbrook was behind me and I didn't want to see it.

"This has got to be a movie," I thought, "this cannot be real. I don't understand killing women and children. I don't understand how the Russian soldiers who liberated Ravensbrook became oppressors for fifty years and now are leaving as friends. I don't understand how Germans whose fathers and grandfathers sank American Navy ships want to play "Anchors Aweigh." And I don't understand how I, having worn a gold ring that belonged to a Jewish child who died somewhere not far from here, can be standing here making sandwiches. I don't understand *any* of it."

One year later, to celebrate our fortieth anniversary, Seymour and I took a trip to British Columbia. We had separate seat assignments on Air Canada, and my two companions were a couple I judged correctly to be ten years older than I am, who spoke what I first thought was Yiddish but soon realized was German.

I felt a dilemma. The book I had packed to read identified me as Jewish and religious. I hesitated, thinking, "These people are Germans." Finally, I read for a while and then put the book down when breakfast was served.

I initiated a conversation with my seatmates. "*Sprechen Sie Englisch?*" "Yes," he said, "I do, but my wife speaks less." They were on holiday now returning to Germany. I told them I had bicycled in Germany and mentioned several trips. When I said "north of Berlin" they were especially eager to talk. "We live near Berlin."

"How was it before the wall came down?" I asked.

"It wasn't as bad as some people think," he said, "if you were careful."

"How old were you when the war ended?" I asked.

"I was seventeen," he said. "I was in a prisoner of war camp in the United States in Georgia. That's where I learned English."

He said tentatively, nodding toward my book, "Many people have trouble going to Germany because of the terrible things that happened there."

I said, "I know that. I was young, nine years old when the war ended. Some relatives who survived came to New York after the war on their way to Canada. I wondered, when I was a child, how I would feel in Germany."

He said, "Before the wall came down, we could only travel in the Eastern bloc nations. Now we go everywhere. Last year we went on a cruise in the Mediterranean. We visited Haifa and Jerusalem. What an experience it was! In the middle of the desert it is green. Israel has really built up something marvelous."

I said, "I remember Israel Independence Day. I was listening on the radio with my family to the vote in the United Nations. I didn't go to Israel until two years ago."

He said, "In the town I grew up in, in Poland, there were almost as many Jews as non-Jews. Everyone did business together. My father had a farm. A Jew came to buy a cow, and they discussed it a long time."

"Uh-oh," I started to think, "is he now going to say something derogatory about Jews bargaining?" I felt tense, but I realized that was not the point of his story. His meaning was "Our communities were separate but bilingual, so we knew how to communicate." He ended by saying, "The cow would be bought. They would drink vodka together, and the next year they would do the same business again."

I thought, "Does he have hidden prejudices? Do I? Am I hearing with skewed sensitivity?"

On the surface the conversation was calm and pleasant. Inside I felt uneasy. I thought of asking, "Were you there when the half of your town that was Jewish was rounded up and shipped off in trains?" I examined my motivation. I decided it wasn't well-intended enough and so I didn't ask. Instead, I said, "I have a friend, a woman who is a rabbi, who went to Auschwitz this year to be part of ceremonies marking fifty years since the liberation."

"I've been there, too," he said. I thought his eyes wavered momentarily, and then returned. "There are a few people these days," he said, "saying those things again, but the press makes more of it than there is. Most people are decent. Even where I grew up, most people were decent."

He spoke about his childhood. He had thirteen brothers and sisters. His wife had nine. "Were you Catholic?" I asked.

"Yes."

"Are you still?"

"Yes, of course. It was not possible to have public services when the regime was there, but since the wall came down we can again. We must remember what happened, we must not forget." I agreed.

We talked about languages. He said he was writing his memoirs. "But," he said, "I'm not sure I can be a writer. To be a writer you need to be interesting to other people."

"I am a writer," I told him.

"What do you write?" he asked

"I've written two books. One is about Buddhism and the other is about Buddhist meditation."

He thought a moment. "Don't you have a problem, a conflict," he said searching for the correct word, "here?" He pointed to his chest, gesturing with both hands as if pulling his heart apart.

"Do you mean," I offered, "is it a problem for me that I am a Jew and also a Buddhist?"

"Yes," he said, "that's what I mean."

"No," I told him, "it's not a problem. I think Judaism and Buddhism speak to each other without conflict, just as you and I are speaking to each other without conflict. We couldn't have been having this conversation fifty years ago."

He said, "When I grew up, the Jews looked different from the rest of us."

"Uh-oh," I froze again, "maybe now he is about to defame, to invoke some stereotype." But he seemed without guile.

"They looked different. They had different clothes"—he gestured at his clothes—"they held themselves apart, their houses smelled different . . . "

I was scanning, thinking, "Is this a statement of fact without hostility, an attempt to understand on his part, or is it unconscious racism?"

I looked down at myself. I was wearing, just because I like to, an ankle-length dark dress, probably not unlike the Jewish women of his Polish town. I had big, heavy, high-top shoes on. I thought they looked like Polish peasant shoes. My hat had a brim covering all my hair. I wasn't wearing makeup. He said, "The Jews in our town looked different. You look just like us."

I extended my arm past his wife to shake hands. "Sylvia Boorstein."

"Freitag," he said, "Richard Freitag. That means Friday."

I said, "*Wiedersehen.*"

He said, "*Das Vidanya.*"

I thought, "One of *my* walls has just come down."

It was a wall I didn't know I had. I think of myself as modern and worldly. I would have said, "I am not a survivor." Perhaps we all are, though. Not just Jews. Everyone who lives in a world where terrible cruelty—variations of holocaust—happens regularly *must* challenge the premise that the natural heart is loving. And the mind in pain balks at the challenge.

Pain confuses the mind, and terrible pain, Holocaust pain, takes a very long time to subside. Jews have been recovering for fifty years. It is very difficult to trust in the natural capacity of the heart to heal and fully love when it is so badly wounded. Even as we are healing, wounding is happening all around us, and as Jews—particularly as Jews—we feel the pain of it. I am frightened by the degree of confusion in the world.

I am *certain* that unconfused mind is loving, but I don't know if we can show enough love to calm enough fear to establish enough clear mind in the time we have to do it. I pray with all my heart that we can.

I think there is a growing respect these days for prayer as part of an awakened, rational life. I think Jews are getting ready to pray again, too, with a calmer heart, with a devotional, hope-filled heart. And these days, it's safe to pray as a Jew.

I took the train from New York to Boston, and the incoming train was late arriving at Penn Station. I stood in a growing mass of people under the track announcement board ready to dash to the escalator. Everyone was facing the same direction, everyone's eyes fixed on the board. "We look like pilgrims venerating a shrine," I thought. Then I spotted a man in a Russian Cossack fur hat, and I thought, "That man is a Jew."

"Track Nine." Everyone ran. The escalator was broken. I trundled down three flights of stairs with what I then realized was an overly heavy suitcase. I wrestled it up into the train and collapsed into the last row, nearest the door, purposely occupying two seats until everyone was settled so I could sit by myself. I thought about saying my prayers, I thought about meditating, and I thought about reading *The*

New York Times. "I could skip the prayers," I thought. "I'm exhausted. I got up too early. I'm not inspired. If I'm not inspired, it won't count."

The train started out, and I noticed a man wearing a *yarmulke* across the aisle, one row ahead of me. Gray hair. Gray mustache. Reading glasses. Turtleneck shirt. *Knitted yarmulke.* "Hip old guy," I thought. "My age." Using his right hand, he pushed the left sleeve of his shirt up over his elbow. I realized he was going to put on *tefillin!* On the train! In front of everybody! He did. I was inspired.

The conductor came down the aisle collecting tickets. He seemed not to notice the *tefillin.* My praying man held his ticket in one hand and his prayer book in the other, and he and the conductor had a brief interchange about train arrival times. Everyone behaved like putting on *tefillin* on a train is a perfectly normal occurrence. The conductor collected my ticket and moved on.

Moments later, the man in the Russian hat showed up. "Do you want my *tallis?*" he asked the man with the knitted *yarmulke.*

"It's okay, thank-you, I'm wearing my *tzitzis* . . . Wait . . . I *would* like a *tallis*, thanks . . . "

The *tallit* was very large—woven wool, beautiful fringes—and the praying man stood up and put it on with smooth, practiced ritual. He sat back down wrapped up in it. I was enjoying participating in the scene. I saw him carefully gather together in one hand the fringes from the four corners of the *tallit* and look at them. From that gesture, I knew exactly where he was in the liturgy, and I felt he and I were praying together.

For a Jew, though, it is not sufficient to feel safe enough to pray. We need to feel safe enough to remember. We need to be able to remember without fear, in the space of clear mind, so that we remember as witnesses rather than as victims. As a victim, I become frightened and then confused and angry. I perpetuate suffering. As a witness, I can testify to the terrible, evil consequences of ignorance and vow to end it. As a witness, I can also swear that my experience of clear mind is one of boundless love and I can teach it. I can respond to suffering, and my response can be compassionate. I can say—with perfect faith—that my contribution to *tikkun olam* (the repair of the world) begins with my dedication to maintaining a loving heart. I can only transform myself. It is all any of us can do. If we all do it, it will be enough.

Tishah B'Av (the ninth day of the month of Av) fell this year on the day after I wrote this chapter. At my morning *minyan*, I remembered that we were speaking blessings and psalms and prayers rather than singing them, because *Tishah B'Av* is a day of mourning. It commemorated, originally, the destruction of the temple in Jerusalem and the exile, but it has come to stand for many destructions in the history of Jews.

The morning service was straightforward: Torah reading from Deuteronomy, a chapter from Jeremiah. Even the chant that accompanies replacing the Torah in its special cabinet after the reading service, "It is a tree of life to all who hold fast to it. Its ways are ways of pleasantness and all its paths are peace," was spoken quietly. We said the *Aleinu* prayer, "It is incumbent upon us to praise God . . . ," and then, as usual, some people sat down as others remained standing for the Mourners' Kaddish.

Most days, just a few people are standing, people commemorating the *yahrzeits* (yearly death anniversaries) of next of kin. I noticed most of the group was standing. Then I remembered that people whose relatives died in the Holocaust, people who did not know the death dates of their kin, recognize *Tishah B'Av* as the *yahrzeits*. My father-in-law, whose parents were shot and then buried in a mass grave in a forest outside Ushetza-Podolsk in the Ukraine, said Kaddish for them on *Tishah B'Av*. I looked at the people who had remained standing and thought, "Can all these people be direct survivors?" Then I realized that we all are, and I stood up too.

V'ahavta—Metta Practice

I don't think it's possible to love God with all your heart and not love everything else. Complete loving mandates and rejoices in complete acceptance. I learned that doing Buddhist *metta* (lovingkindness) meditation.

Metta practice is concentration practice. The practitioner attempts to develop specially deepened concentration by steadfastly focusing attention on one single object. One form of *metta* practice uses a set of resolves, wishes for the well-being (safety, health, and happiness) of all living things.

One set of formal resolves is:

> May all beings be safe.
> May all beings be healthy.
> May all beings be happy.
> May all beings live with ease.

The *metta* practitioner attempts to keep the resolves as the ongoing focus of attention. Some practitioners repeat the resolves silently, internally. Others say them aloud, alone or with a group. I sing mine to myself. I use a melody of special emotional significance to me that scans exactly with the words of the formal *metta* resolves I recite. Full *metta* practice includes dedication to maintaining a friendly, noncombative attitude in all conditions, even those that preclude recitation of resolves. I think of it as benevolence practice.

When I began my own *metta* practice, I thought I was constructing some new, *special* capacity for experiencing peace. What I discovered was that one-pointed, focused concentration causes greed, anger, and confusion to disappear. When I'm being exuberant I say, "We discover the loving, friendly, compassionate, generous, kind beings that we actually are." The simplest thing to say is "the wisdom of the natural mind is revealed."

Metta practice is transformative. The direct experience of the pleasure—indeed, the joy—of benevolence, over time, lessens the habitual self-centered, defensive actions of the mind and strengthens the habit of friendly acceptance. Responsive behavior—motivated by kindness—replaces reactive behavior. Benevolent, decisive, strong responses are possible. We become peaceful, passionate people.

Formal *metta* practice begins with wishing well to the people nearest and dearest—people toward whom wishing well comes naturally. The delight that arises in the mind from thinking about well-loved teachers, friends, and family prepares the way for wishing well to what is called, in Buddhist Scripture, "the enemy." The mechanics of transformation are presented scientifically. As the mind focuses, rapture arises. Rapture is the natural antidote to antipathy. We don't *forget* that our enemies caused us pain. We don't necessarily decide to be involved with them further. Discerning awareness remains while anger disappears. We remember, "This person acted terribly; we must never allow these kinds of actions; we must teach each other, and our children, only kindness; we must never forget, so that we remain committed to morality and justice." We remember without rancor.

In *metta* practice, the effort to maintain steadfast benevolence is rewarded with the discovery that benevolence is the essence of the natural mind and is, in fact, effortless. When we are fully present, we are naturally kind. What I am teaching most these days is the possibility of living an alert, engaged, unembittered life.

When people begin *metta* practice, they ignore particular angers and aversions and focus on people they feel eager to love. They begin by thinking, "Okay, I'll love these people, but I'll never forgive So-and-so who hurt me so much." Ultimately they discover that half measures are not possible. The joy-filled freedom of loving diminishes and ultimately erases the power of painful experience. Anger gives way to compassion. Life is forgiven for being painful.

"*V'ahavta* . . . And you shall love—the Lord your God with all your heart, with all your soul, and with all your strength" is, I think, the *metta* practice of Judaism. The phrase itself, the mandate to be completely loving, begins the first sentence of a prayer recited twice daily in formal liturgy. The rest of the prayer, however, makes clear that the practice of loving completely is a constant one that should be maintained from "rising up" to "lying down," from "sitting at home" to "walking on the way"; that it should frame and inform your speech; and that symbolic reminders of dedication to loving should be used to strengthen resolve.

> And you shall love God with all your heart, with all your soul, and with all your strength. Take these words to heart. Teach them to your children. Speak of them when you sit in your house, when you walk on the road, when you lie down and when you get up. Bind them as a sign upon your hand, keep them visible before your eyes. Inscribe them on your doorposts and your gates.

The second and third paragraphs of the *V'ahavta* prayer, not included in all prayer books, read literally as an admonition to keep the commandment to love God so that rain will fall and crops will grow. I read them as "Nothing can jeopardize you when you love completely."

When the heart is noncombative, when it is peaceful—which only happens when it is loving—the mind is clear. Wisdom prevails. We understand painful things happen because that's the way life is. Complete God-love, clear mind, allows us to forgive life. The possibility of steadfast loving allows life—whatever its particulars—to always remain a gift.

Compassion Is Compassion

THE DALAI LAMA TAUGHT A WEEKLONG RESIDENTIAL
course on Patience to twelve hundred people in a hotel outside of Tucson in 1993. His text was chapter six of
Shantideva's *Guide to the Bodhisattva's Way of Life,* which he
explicated word by word, verse by verse. The single, central,
reiterated message was the value of restraint and reflection
whenever vexation fills the mind. People were thrilled by
the clarity of his teachings. Mostly, though, they had come
to watch him. They wanted to experience being in a room
with him. They wanted "to see how the rebbe ties his
shoes."

Just before the lunch break on the last day of the course,
the Dalai Lama announced that he would offer the Green
Tara Initiation that afternoon as the ritual closing of the
course. The Green Tara Initiation is a special blessing
based on Green Tara, a female deity who embodies compassion, and the Blessing/Initiation is meant to arouse a
sense of compassion. It is a guided visualization in which
participants hope to realize their own capacity for compassion.

A questioner in the back of the room raised his hand.

"I am a practicing Catholic, and I am worried about
doing an initiation. What do you think? Is it all right for me
to do it?"

The Dalai Lama paused thoughtfully and then said, "I
think it's all right. If anything comes along that is uncomfortable for you, don't do it."

Two hours later the whole group reassembled as usual to await the Dalai Lama's entrance and stood up in formal welcome as he made his way to the dais, bowed three times to the Buddha, and arranged himself on his seat. In complete silence, twelve hundred people sat down to begin the ceremony. The Dalai Lama, in a conversational tone, said, "I've been thinking further about the question of doing the initiation if you belong to another spiritual tradition. I think you can do it." He gave a list of reasons, explaining slowly and carefully, saying essentially that "compassion is compassion" and "a blessing is a blessing." Then he did the Green Tara Initiation.

Roberta Goldfarb, a Zen teacher, said it took her six-and-a-half years to get ready to bow in front of a statue of the Buddha. "I'm a Jew, so bowing was a hard thing for me to do. In the beginning I refused to bow; for years I stood there while everyone else bowed. One day, after years of practice, I cautiously experimented with bowing, to see what came up.

"One day I remembered 'just bowing.' Everything that had been attached to the action dropped away, and I 'just bowed.' It was so freeing . . . it was one of the high points of my entire Zen practice."

Roberta's daughter Sarah attends a Hebrew Day School, and one of the teachers questioned Roberta about a *sesshin* (a Zen meditation retreat) she was thinking about attending.

"I just need to be reassured that you aren't praying to the Buddha."

I asked Roberta, "What did you say?"

Roberta said, "I told her it isn't praying."

"Did you tell her," I asked, "that the Buddha would have been shocked to have people pray to him? Did you tell her that in the teaching to the people of Kalama he said, 'Don't trust anyone, even a Buddha, to tell you what truth is. Experience it for yourself'? Did you also say that the Buddha said, in his final words, 'Everyone can do this, but everyone needs to do it for themselves.'?"

"No," Roberta said, "I just said it isn't praying. That's enough."

Not long ago, I was a panelist at a conference in Philadelphia and I said, "Since my Buddhist meditation practice is bare-bones-just-sitting mindfulness, it has not been ritually challenging." Rabbi Zalman Schachter-Shalomi responded, "Maybe we need a *hechsher* (a rabbinical sanction) for what is okay to do."

I said, relieved that our presentation time was running over, "Perhaps we can take this up in the afternoon session."

The dining room was crowded at lunchtime—there were 450 people at the conference—but one woman made an effort to find me and was eager to talk. She was worried. She said, "I've come all the way from Wisconsin to hear this particular discussion, please do *not* let Reb Zalman make a ruling on which practices are kosher and which are *treif* (forbidden). I've been doing Tibetan practice for years. I do bowing. I say a mantra. And I feel myself more dedicated and devout as a Jew than ever."

Halachah (Jewish law) did not come up at the afternoon panel. There were more panelists and a different agenda. But the issue exists. I think it will continue to exist—at least for a while—until enough people are reassured.

A rabbi in Jerusalem, part of the traditionally orthodox community, talked with me on several occasions about my meditation practice and about what I teach. In a recent meeting I told him about this book, and he was genuinely interested. I said, "I'm very glad you've been willing to talk about Buddhism with me."

"Of course I am, why not?"

"Well, sometimes people worry about '*Avodah Zarah* (idol worship) . . . '"

"I don't know enough about what you do to know if it is. I *need* to listen to you."

"So, can I tell that in my book? Just that you were willing to listen?"

"Yes, sure."

"Can I tell your name?"

"No, don't tell my name. Someone might think I was saying that it is definitely kosher what you are doing. It might be. It might not be."

The rabbi's remark was not dismissive. I felt it as genuine uncertainty. He didn't know enough.

At other times I think the alarm people express about Buddhism has more to do with instinctive fears about tribal survival than philosophic error. Perhaps that's why *ha-lachah* becomes an issue. Although for me it is not the central criterion for identity, it seems to be a visible reassuring cue, "Okay, that person is still *in*." Conversely, any academic *interest* in another tribe and philosophical discourse *about* another tribe might not be worrisome. But doing an *action* that another group does—sitting on a meditation cushion, lighting incense, any action more familiar to another community than to one's own—arouses concern. I think it's the natural, self-protective, genetic response of tribes.

Buddhism is not a tribe. I once read a response by Thich Nhat Hanh, a noted contemporary Vietnamese Buddhist teacher, to the question, "Would you kill a person under *any* circumstances? What if that person were about to kill the last Buddhist on earth?"

His response was, "I wouldn't. It wouldn't matter if it was the last Buddhist on earth. If there is any truth, any value to Buddhism, it would come back again."

His was a philosophic answer. It wasn't a family answer. It wasn't a tribe answer.

I have tribal pride (and sometimes tribal dismay) in ways that feel like family responses. I had a moment of tribal alarm several years ago while having lunch in the staff dining room during a mindfulness retreat. Someone, a Jew, said, "It's too bad that Judaism is dying as a religion. It's so quaint." I didn't say anything—it was a gentle remark, a casual musing, not directed at me in particular and not unkind in tone. I was surprised, though, by the intensity of my internal response. I wasn't angry. I was frightened. "No, it *isn't* dying," I thought. "It is *not!*" I remember the sense of arousal that accompanied my fear, and I wondered afterwards whether that's what's meant by the phrase "defender of the faith."

It was fine with me that the rabbi in Jerusalem was hesitant about the propriety of my practice. I considered it part of his job. I loved it that he listened. When I left my interview with him, he wished me well in my teaching, and when I asked for a blessing for my writing, he was happy to offer one.

The Great Way Is Not Difficult

THE FIRST MINDFULNESS RETREAT FOR RABBIS I TAUGHT
was held at the Barre Center for Buddhist Studies. I looked
forward to it with more than casual pleasure. The particular
rabbis who were invited had expressed interest in meditation and I was glad to be teaching them in Barre, where I
had done so much of my own practice.

I was worried about the presence of the Buddha statue
in the meditation hall. The room itself is sparsely fur-
nished. It has white walls, a vaulted ceiling, large windows
that look out into rural Massachusetts. There are twenty
sets of meditation mats topped by meditation cushions—
zabutons and *zafus*—lined up in four rows facing a table
with a Buddha statue on it and an image of the Buddha on
a wall-hanging, a *tanka*, behind it. The *tanka* and the
Buddha are in the direct line of vision of anyone opening
the front door of the building even before they enter the
meditation room.

My friend Sheila and I have taught a mindfulness retreat
for Jews each fall for several years in Barre. The precursor of
our retreats were Jewish-Buddhist *dialogues*, usually on
Sundays. Jews and Buddhists met to discuss complementar-
ities and convergences in both traditions. When it seemed
clear that people had come not for dialogue but to be reassured that practicing meditation and studying Buddhism
was okay and to experience rather than talk—we shifted to a
retreat model, a mindfulness retreat for Jews. Retreatants
arrived on Thursday, practiced mindfulness meditation in
silence until Friday evening, and then celebrated Shabbat

with ritual, liturgy, Torah reading, and study. On Sunday everyone talked about their experience.

Once the retreat had become a Jewish experience—informed by Dharma, of course, but essentially a Jewish experience—the statue of the Buddha became a problem. For one thing, there were logistical difficulties. Sheila needed a place to put her Torah. We found a table for the Torah, put it in place under the *tanka*, and pushed the Buddha on his table into the corner of the room. Mu Soeng, the director of the Study Center, watched us do it.

Sheila said to me, "Say something to Mu Soeng. I'm not sure he approves."

I said, "Mu Soeng, this is a test of your nonattachment."

Mu Soeng seemed relaxed about his test. We moved the Buddha. Actually, I think *I* failed the "attachment test." I was attached—caught, held captive—by my fear that the statue would make Jews uncomfortable, and I wanted them to be comfortable. The Buddha statue had never bothered me in my years of practice—I experienced him as a benevolent presence—but the term *Avodah Zarah* (idol worship) was one I had been hearing from Jews questioning Buddhism.

The following year, when Sheila and I arrived to prepare for our retreat, Mu Soeng's assistant said, "Mu Soeng wants you to leave the Buddha in front. He says you can put the Torah next to it."

I felt an unaccustomed flash of anger. I like Mu Soeng very much. He and I are good friends, and when I'm in Barre we always spend time talking. I like to run ideas by him for review. He has a completely sensible Zen mind and points out when my thinking is deluded.

"How could Mu Soeng do this to us?" I thought. "*Why* would he do this? Is he really that attached? He *knows* these are all Jews, many of them Jews struggling with religious identity crises. I don't need to stir up their minds, create extra problems. They have enough problems. I want them to calm *down*."

Fortunately, I thought about my unusual anger. Actually, I was mindful of it. "What's happening?" I asked myself. "*I'm frightened* is what's happening. I'm frightened that these arriving students will become upset, that they will have a bad time, that they will give Sheila and me a hard time, that it's unnecessary trouble." My anger disappeared. We put the Torah on a table in the corner and turned all the meditation cushions ninety degrees so everyone would be looking out the windows instead of at the Buddha or the Torah.

I said to Sheila, "This is, anyway, more appropriate. We are facing east." The following year Sheila and I co-led the rabbi retreat. The retreat was held during the week, so we had no Torah. We decided to put the Buddha, with his table, in the closet. Once again, we turned the seats to face east, away from the *tanka*.

On the last morning of the retreat, people shared their experience. I shared mine—my complete, indeed blown-away, beyond-words pleasure at being able to share understandings so dear to me with people, with Jews, so willing to learn. At some point Sheila told the ongoing saga of the Buddha statue. Someone asked, "Where is he?"

"He's in there," Sheila replied, pointing.

Someone said, "You didn't need to put the Buddha in the closet."

A *Beit Knesset* Is Not Supposed to Be a *Zendo*

I WAS FORTY YEARS OLD WHEN I WAS INTRODUCED TO Buddhist meditation, and I was surprised to find how much I loved monastic life. Some of my friends were surprised by my new schedule—going off at regular intervals for a week or two of "sitting."

"You *like* that?"

"How can you *stand* not talking?"

"No *reading* either? I'd go crazy! What do you *do* all day?"

I didn't try to explain a lot—I'm not sure, retrospectively, that I understood it myself, and anyway I was at the older edge of the wave of new meditators in the 1970s and my friends were generally too old to be "hip."

I think it was inevitable that Jews studying Buddhism and discovering the tranquillity, orderliness, and seriousness of meditation retreats would compare these new religious experiences with synagogue experiences. Jewish meditators routinely told me:

"No one sits quietly in *shul*!"

"We had a fifteen-second silent reflection, and then the music started. I couldn't even decide whom I was going to pray *for*, much less pray!"

"People are coming and going all the time."

"I don't believe in a God."

"The liturgy is sexist."

"There is nothing *spiritual* going on there."

I'd had some of those same thoughts myself.

A number of years had passed between my being an active member of a synagogue community and the beginning of my meditation practice. I wasn't looking for a new community. My family and friends and professional life were *full* of people whom I loved. I was looking for a practice. Indeed, the fact that retreats are *not* interactive was (and is) a great allure. I find the presence of other meditators a sustaining structure—my discipline in keeping the retreat schedule is silently supported by meditators around me practicing the same form in the same space. I was delighted to discover what a relief it is to be able to depend on everyone to leave me alone. Retreatants don't make eye contact. I feel I am being respected. I feel that everyone has said, "I know you can do this!"

Monasteries appeal to me. I've never been to Asia to practice meditation, and I've never spent many consecutive months intensively practicing in this country as many of my friends have. But I might have, had my life circumstances been different, because I love the quiet, the simplicity, and both the peacefulness of the contented, focused mind and the sometimes surprising (albeit temporal) bliss, rapture, and fireworks (yes indeed, *even* sitting, *especially* sitting still) of the radically clear mind. The monastic path, however, was never an option for me. I had a husband and four children when I discovered meditation—now I have grandchildren—and family life is *also* very appealing to me. I've tried to interpolate retreat practice into my family's schedule skillfully. It's been a bit like carrying a double major in college. When I think of all the retreats I've been part of over the last twenty years—a week here, two weeks there, ten days, and sometimes a whole month at a time—I think, "At *least* two years, maybe three, if I added it all up."

Some practice periods have been harder than others; they've all been different, but one experience has been consistent. At any retreat, anywhere, two or three days into the silence, I feel my mind (and my body) relax. "Aaaah," I think, "This is *it*. This is the proper way to live. In a graceful, cooperative, silent community. I wish I could stay here forever." Then, some time later—days, sometimes weeks—I begin to think about my family again and feel enthusiastic about resuming my relational life and my work life. Most often the transition back to regular life has been easy. The first few days are interesting—everyone seems busier and noisier than I remember—but I try to make the adjustment part of my practice. After all, an attachment to silence and slowness would be another attachment and would mean more suffering. I do love retreat practice, though, and I love teaching retreat discipline. And a year ago I joined a local synagogue.

Joining a synagogue after a twenty-year absence seems like it might mark some particular event—a particular insight, or even a particular birthday. That wasn't my experience. Belonging or not belonging for two decades had not been an issue. I didn't think about it. Synagogue membership seems yet another aspect of my current life, like prayers and Sabbath observance, that was absent for a while and has now become important. Each renewed practice has seemed timely. "Oh yes, I guess this *is* what I want to do." I never felt an obligation.

When I think about the forms of Jewish practice that have reentered my life I see—or at least I *think* I see—how they built on each other and how they were inspired by my monastic Buddhist meditation practice. Practicing mindfulness I felt peaceful and happy. Feeling peaceful and happy caused me to say blessings. Saying blessings reminded me of prayers, which I had found comforting as a child, and inspired me to pray again. My meditation experiences, especially those that presented themselves in terms of Scripture imagery, reminded me to read Scripture again. At some point I adjusted my reading schedule to the weekly Torah portion. I'm fairly sure my Sabbath observance is a direct consequence of my monastic practice. The possibility of a regularly scheduled day set aside for mindful recollection, meditation, and study—one that I could ritually celebrate with my family—is compelling.

Joining a local synagogue came later. I wasn't "holding out," I just wasn't *drawn*. I'm not a very groupy person, and besides, my immediate family is fifteen people and that already is a *minyan*. My children are grown and have their own families. I do political action/service work with my Spirit Rock community, and I sit with them weekly. I teach meditation retreats many weeks a year. I didn't feel a need.

Things change. Desire arises. Everything conditions (influences) everything else. As a consequence of my revitalized commitment to Judaism, Seymour and I began spending a month each year in Jerusalem. For a person with a study practice, who lives in rural California, Jerusalem is amazing. It seemed to us that everyone there was studying something with someone whom they were eager for us to meet. The study atmosphere—at least among my friends there—is intense enough to have led us on one occasion to fly to Eilat to relax and sit on the beach for three days just to catch our breath.

I think that ultimately it was the diversity of prayer scenes in Jerusalem that enabled me to recognize something about communal worship that I hadn't recognized before. I sat by myself at the Wall. I sat with women behind a screen at Beth Israel in Yemin Moshe and with women in a room *adjoining* the prayer room of the Breslover synagogue in Katamon, listening to liturgy through a transom window. I sat next to Seymour at Kol HaNeshamah (the Renewal congregation where Levi Weiman-Kelman is the rabbi). What I recognized was an insight about form. Once I had it, I knew that finding a prayer community nearer home was the next step.

Everything that we choose to do is a form. Form isn't who we *are* or the goal of what we hope to achieve. Form is just form. I want to be a completely kind and loving person, and I believe my forms support that goal. Congregational Jewish worship is one of my forms.

My form insight consolidated during a Shabbat service at the West London Reform Synagogue. Seymour and I were spending Shabbat in London en route home from Jerusalem, and the West London Reform was nearest to our hotel. It was different from anything I'd seen in Jerusalem or anything I knew in America. The rabbis wore black robes with white collars that made them look like Anglican clergy. The choir sang, in British-accented Hebrew, melodies that sounded like Protestant hymns. The architecture of the building was gothic, with perhaps a touch of a mosque feeling of pillars and arches. The women wore big hats, lots of makeup, and such short skirts that my modesty meter, having been set to Jerusalem standards, registered alarm over so much leg exposure. But the bar mitzvah celebrant read Torah and discussed it: "When I grow up I want to be a barrister so I can be just like Moses and decide what's right and what's wrong." And we said, more or less, the same prayers that I regularly say and enjoy. I thought, "I am connected to the form *inside* this form." I love the sound of the prayer words, and I always feel a rush of excitement when someone picks up the Torah after the weekly reading, and the congregation sings, "*Zot haTorah . . .*" (This is the Torah).

The week after the West London Reform Sabbath, Seymour and I spent Shabbat morning at Congregation Beth Ami in Santa Rosa, California, a conservative synagogue in the nearest city to our rural home. It seemed, using Buddhist terminology, quite "middle path." Men and women sit together. The prayer book is Sim Shalom, the regular prayer book of the conservative movement, and prayer versions that include references to the matriarchs—Sarah, Rebekka, Rachel, and Leah—are pasted onto the inside cover. The cantor is a woman who plays guitar and the *Musaf* (additional) service was sung to Debbie Friedman melodies. A Shlomo Carlebach melody showed up, unexpectedly, in the middle of the *Ahavah Rabah* prayer in the *Shacharit* (morning) liturgy.

It was a somewhat hectic bar mitzvah morning. Seymour and I sat in the middle of the last pew. On Seymour's left was a man older than he is who started late, but being a fluent pray-er, caught up. On my right was a boy of about ten reading a paperback novel, *Fear City*. On his right were two younger boys reading and exchanging Garfield cartoon books. The early arrivals worked steadfastly through the preliminary blessings, although the whole scene was somewhat unsettled as people arrived late, greeted one another, found seats, found their places in the prayer book. For the most part, the congregation seemed at home with the liturgy and knew the tunes. Everyone seemed relaxed.

The service lasted three hours. A boy named Josh was the bar mitzvah celebrant and chanted his Torah portion as well as a very long reading from the prophet Ezekiel. His grandparents and religious school teachers all took turns saying, publicly, how proud they were of him. Babies cried and were taken out and brought back in again, sleeping. Young people took old people on walkers back and forth to the toilet. Some women—I guessed they were part of Josh's family—left before the service finished, probably to prepare the reception in the social hall. The rabbi's sermon emphasized moral choices. Josh's religious school class—fifteen boys and girls—all crowded behind him as the congregation sang the final hymn and threw candy over him. I asked Seymour, "Did people throw candy on you at your bar mitzvah?"

"Yeah, they did. People in the congregation threw little bags of candy."

"Did you like it?"

"I liked that it meant it was all over. It was an ordeal for me. But I was a nervous kid. Josh looks like he's enjoying it."

Josh *did* look like he was enjoying it. There was a big party in the social hall afterward, but we chose not to stay. We were visitors and didn't know anyone. The rabbi greeted us as we left. "Come back any time," he said, "especially when there isn't a bar mitzvah. We have a dairy potluck lunch together." We did. We joined. It was no big deal. Everything turns out to be easier than we think.

I'm thinking a lot these days about different practices for different venues.

Someone said to me recently, after a particularly busy Sabbath morning service, "It's hard to have a spiritual experience here." I was touched by his remark, and its wistful tone, because I thought I knew what he meant and what he felt he was missing.

The synagogue had been unusually crowded that morning. In addition to the bar mitzvah celebrant and his extended family, a longtime member of the congregation was being honored on her eightieth birthday, and four old women, clearly her friends who had come for the occasion, had been sitting in the row in front of mine. Liturgy notwithstanding, they had kept up a running conversation.

My initial—never mind initial—my *ongoing* response to the chatting women had been a simultaneous attempt to connect with the language of prayer while noticing, and restraining, the impulse to join the alternative *minyan* that conducts prayer services without *b'nai mitzvah* and without birthdays in a room across the courtyard. At some point I realized that my attempt had not only been fruitless, it had also been ridiculous. I pray that I will be a loving person. I want to have a completely open heart. *And* I had allowed myself to get caught up in pouting, sanctimonious irritation with the chatting women because they had prevented me from saying words. I stopped saying words. I practiced loving them. I thought, "This is far out! These women have made it to eighty years old—more or less sound of mind and body—this is *really* 'Thanks, God.' Everything else is just words." I also thought, "Now I am doing *metta* (loving-kindness) meditation in my *shul*. I love you, eighty-year-old women."

Am I disparaging Judaism by saying it's just a form? I don't think so. It *is* just a form. Everything that we can speak about is just a form.

Judaism is a wonderful form for me. It's also convenient. It's a form whose vocabulary is familiar to me, one that fits the cultural style and community in which I choose to live. It's a form that I am delighted to share with my children and grandchildren. It's a form that has been able to grow and shift and accommodate and absorb enough to have survived for four thousand years. Within it I find imagery and poetry and ancestry and continuity that nourish me.

Jewish in Jerusalem

IT'S OFTEN COMPLICATED FOR ME NOT TO FEEL
challenged as a Jew in Jerusalem. Some parts are wonderful, of course. I am thrilled each time I see the Magen
David flag flying on top of the Knesset building. I remember sitting on the floor in our living room in Brooklyn, in
front of the Magnavox radio speaker in 1948, listening to
the partition vote in the United Nations. "Paraguay votes
'yes.'" My mother started to cry. The radio switched to "live
in Tel-Aviv," and, through a lot of static, we could hear people singing *"Hatikvah."* Seeing how Jews have built a beautiful, bountiful democracy in the middle of a desert, in the
midst of enemies, makes me proud. And, completely at the
least-essential end of the spectrum of what is important in
life, being in Israel is a great treat for me since I am (after a
several decades' hiatus) once again *kashrut* observant, and
Jerusalem has great restaurants.

Being a devotional Jew in Jerusalem is harder. Seymour
likes to join Rabbi Sheinberger's *minyan* at the Wall for
prayer services, but the women's side is dismal. There is an
ordinance (not posted but understood) against women
praying together, so there is none of the pleasure of communal chanting and no group ritual. I enjoy bowing, saying
"We bend and bow and thank" in concert with other people. Also, I keep needing to remember where I am in rela-
tion to external geography. I need to know if I am at the
Wall, or in Rabbi Sheinberger's home, or at Kol
HaNeshamah, or in Tel-Aviv, or on the beach in Eilat, so I

can choose which clothing to put on or take off so I can "look like the other Jews."

My neighbors in Yemin Moshe, Americans from Seattle, my age, invited us for the Third Meal on the Sabbath. The women wore hats indoors, and the conversation focused on degrees of ritual observance. In spite of the cordial hospitality, I was tense, anticipating their inevitable questions: "Are your children married to Jews?" and "What line of work are you in?" How would I say, "No, but they are married to wonderful people," and "I teach Buddhist meditation"? I wished they would ask, "How do you love God these days?" or "How are you doing on loving people these days?" or "How much compassion practice do you do every day?" These are questions I could relate to. Every day my answers would be different, and I would be able to explain my ideas of spiritual practice.

It's also more challenging for me to be a Buddhist in Dharamsala than in Berkeley. In Dharamsala I watched people whirling handheld prayer wheels, or walking alongside a bank of huge prayer wheels, spinning the wheels as they walked, reciting prayers, and thought, "I don't do that." Sometimes, not often, I wondered what that means about my Buddhism. It is a style of practice, but it isn't what the Buddha taught. Mostly, my challenge in ritual situations is relational—how to behave without causing discomfort to others and/or to myself. So, in Jerusalem, I steer the potentially upsetting conversations into subjects that are neutral. In Dharamsala I nod, or do a respectful "*Namaste*" (palms touching at chest) gesture, to people who acknowledge me.

In situations where I feel ritually challenged, when I *am* uncomfortable, I often think, "Take me to a *zendo*!" It's my shorthand for "Let's just sit quietly together." And, sitting quietly in Buddhist retreats, I often think, "*Hiney mah tov umah na'im . . .* (How good and how pleasant it is to sit together)."

Dinner Party in Jerusalem

JERUSALEM FEELS TO ME LIKE AN ETERNAL SPIRITUAL crossroads. I've had experiences there that felt like a preview of the world to come. One of those was a Shabbat dinner on Friday evening, January 5, 1996. Seymour and I were guests at Menachem and Batya Kallus's apartment in Bakaa. All the guests were Jews, and all of us, in varying degrees, were knowledgeable about Buddhism. Everyone knew that tools of practice are just tools of practice and names of paths are just names of paths. "What are your goals?" and "How do you know you're making progress?" were our understood points of convergence.

Menachem sat at the head of the table. At his left was Seymour, I came next, at my left was Yael Bentor, a Tibetologist, and, at her left, Moshe Siev. At the foot of the table was Moshe's son Jedediah, and at his left Yossi Chajes, a doctoral student, followed by his two daughters Keturah and Levanah, ages two and four, and then Menachem's wife, Batya. Everyone had a story. Here they are.

Menachem

Menachem, on that Shabbat evening, had just gotten back from Boston where he had presented a paper at the Academy of Jewish Studies attempting to show that the Baal Shem Tov had been influenced by the prayer practices taught by Isaac Luria. Menachem is finishing his doctorate at Hebrew University, studying with Professor Moshe Idel. His area of study is the interpolation of Lurianic Kabbalah with the Tantric teachings of Namkhai Norbu.

I met Menachem the first time I was in Israel, but he told me his spiritual odyssey only three days before the dinner party. We spent several hours together sharing our stories.

"I started looking around at other religions after I left the yeshiva for the third time."

"Menachem," I laughed, startled, "I can see you are nothing if not dogged."

"Why do you say that?"

"Nobody leaves the yeshiva *three* times."

"Well, I kept going back, hoping . . . "

Much of Menachem's story has a *Raiders of the Lost Ark* quality about it, and I kept thinking, as he told his tale into the January twilight, "This would make a *great* movie!" He described his trip down the Amazon in Peru, at age twenty-one, to study indigenous religions and explained how a piece of misinformation about a tribal location had left him marooned for three days and nights in the jungle. "I then became," Menachem said, "the first person in the Upper Amazon Basin to put on *tefillin* while reading Padmasambhava's *Book of the Great Liberation*."

Menachem's story continued with his against-all-odds rescue through more years of searching until, in Berkeley, because a "friend couldn't go to a retreat he had signed up for and offered me his place," he met Namkhai Norbu, a Tibetan lama, who taught *dzogchen* and introduced Menachem to "the View."

Apt *dzogchen* practitioners (usually people who have done preliminary practices to strengthen concentration) are able, given timely initiatory instructions by a *dzogchen* master, to experience nonseparateness (emptiness), to realize the nature of the mind as spacious. Qualities such as lovingkindness, compassion, spontaneous joy, and equanimity are then seen clearly to be natural rather than constructed states, and remaining in them becomes relatively easy. Menachem credits this discovery, and his ability to intentionally invoke altered mind states, with being fundamental to his prayer life and a key component of his continuing practice as a devout Jew.

In conversation, Menachem speaks modern Hebrew. For blessings, he uses the Ashkenazi Hebrew of Brooklyn yeshivas. As I watched him preside at the Shabbat table and listened to him chant, I imagined him as his grandfather in Poland.

Yael

Yael is an Israeli. Her doctorate is in Tibetology, and she teaches Tibetan, Sanskrit, and Buddhism at Hebrew University on the Mount Scopus campus. Her husband, also a Tibetologist, was spending the year in Oslo, working with a select group of six scholars translating some recently discovered Tibetan texts. Yael became interested in Buddhism when she traveled in India as a young adult. She said that traveling in India is still quite a common practice among young Israelis—ten thousand of them make the trip each year—just after they finish their compulsory army service and before university. Yael said that most young people go as travelers, not seekers. Some, like herself, become more deeply interested.

I recalled, as Yael spoke, that Seymour and I had once spent a Shabbat afternoon in Efrat visiting at the home of an American family that had made *aliyah* (emigrated permanently) to Israel twenty years ago. They were worried because one of their sons, nearing the end of his army service, was considering a trip to Thailand and India. To them, as orthodox Jews, his interest in a Buddhist country was frightening. I remembered thinking, as I listened to their concern, that their son's proposed trip did not sound like an intentional spiritual search. I had said, "It's probably just about having an experience of traveling abroad." I'd hoped that their visit with me, knowing that I was a Buddhist teacher and seeing that I was a Jew, would reassure them in case their son's trip did become a spiritual search. I think that was more than they were ready to consider. As I listened to Yael, I wondered what had happened to the young man from Efrat.

Moshe

Moshe Siev's father was a rabbi and his grandfather was a rabbi and his great-grandfather was one of the important founders of Israel. There is a street in Jerusalem named after him. Moshe left Judaism after graduating from Yeshiva University and (to the considerable distress of his parents) made furniture, studied Gurdjieff, met and became friends with Jon Kabat-Zinn and Larry Rosenberg (now a teacher at Cambridge Insight Meditation Center), who introduced him to John Bennett, his Gurdjieff teacher, and at thirty-six went back to medical school. Moshe is a pediatrician. He and his wife, Amy, have three children and live in New Haven.

I met Moshe at a Jewish-Buddhist conference at Barre two years before we met again in Jerusalem. He told me then that he had rediscovered Judaism as his spiritual path following his first mindfulness meditation retreat at the Insight Meditation Society. He said the experience of the retreat was one of powerful spiritual intimacy. His reconnection with Judaism happened during the Rosh Hashanah service following that first mindfulness retreat. Moshe said "Now I am very happy to have had the intense Jewish education I had because I can read texts, and I don't have to start from the very beginning in order to learn."

There was a magic *tikkun* in the fact that Moshe was in Jerusalem visiting Jed when we were there. During the week preceding that Shabbat, Seymour and I had dinner with Moshe, and they discovered that Moshe's father, Asher Siev, had been the main nemesis of Seymour's parochial education, indeed the person that Seymour most connects with his leaving Yeshiva High School fifty years ago. Moshe had arranged an audience with the Amshanover Rebbe for the very next day, and so Seymour went with him. They both received blessings, and Seymour was profoundly moved by his, which he continues to feel is acting in him. The rebbe, hearing that Seymour was a doctor, said, "I bless you that you should be able to love your patients very much."

Jedediah
Jed Siev, *Yedidya* (beloved of God), was spending one year before college "learning" in a Yeshiva in Jerusalem. Jed graduated from Maimonides High School in Boston where he was student body president, an athlete, a very good scholar. He is tall, good looking, charming. He entered into discussions of texts, source materials, references, and meanings with complete ease. He was one of the discussants at the dinner table—not an awkward teenager eager to get on to do something else. He didn't hesitate to correct his father, or amplify some point that his father made, but his

additions were entirely easy, just two thinkers thinking— not a father and son at odds with each other. Moshe loved it. He was clearly *kvell*ing (experiencing parental pride).

Yossi

Yossi is a Fulbright Scholar doing his doctorate at Hebrew University, studying sixteenth-century writings about dybbuks. His two- and four-year-old daughters were with him. His newborn baby and his wife were in America visiting grandparents. Yossi mentioned that he had spent the day "browsing in bookstores with Idel." Everyone wanted to know what each of them had bought.

Yossi's father had emigrated to Palestine from Austria, and then to the United States in 1938. Yossi said, "My father was intensely Jewish but not at all religious, so I had no early religious background. He was a pianist and a composer, though," Yossi added, "and I think his spirituality expressed itself in his music."

Describing his own awakening to Judaism as a spiritual path, Yossi told about spending time at Swami Muktananda's *ashram* in Ann Arbor when he was at school, as well as "at any other thing that was coming around." He said that he dropped out of the University of Michigan after one year and "spent a year in Los Angeles and met Jonathan Omer-Man, who introduced me to Judaism as a path, and here I am."

"Let's back up a minute," I said. "Can you tell me why you were in Muktananda's *ashram* in the first place?"

"Yes, of course. I was passionately looking for God, and I was looking everywhere."

"Why were you looking? Were you doing that the year before?"

"No. I don't think so. The year before I was just thinking about college. Some hard things happened to me. I got
in trouble for my political activism, and it made me dis-
couraged and pessimistic. Then I started looking for God.
But of course," Yossi added, "this is just what I am telling
you this moment. The truth is that the story changes each
time I tell it. Not because any of the facts aren't true. All the
facts are true. What seems *important* changes through time.
I would be telling this differently a year ago, and probably it
will be different a year from now. There were surely things
in my childhood, seeds that set the scene for the search, but
it was just at that time that the search manifested."

Keturah and Levanah jostled each other and played
throughout the evening. They spent more time doing som-
ersaults on the sofa behind the table than sitting at the
table. They fell down, they cried, they climbed on and off
Yossi to be comforted. They also washed hands and said
blessings in line with everyone else and sat still to receive
the traditional blessing for children from their father.

Batya

Batya Cohen grew up in Boston in the early years of the
Jewish Renewal movement and was active in some of the
first Jewish feminist groups. She is an Israeli citizen now,
working as a consultant to progressive spiritual and political organizations. She was one of the Women at the Wall
protesting the ban against women praying together.

Batya and Menachem's household is one of strict *ha-
lachic* observance, a taken-for-granted, natural part of their
lives as religious, spiritual people. Menachem said the
blessing over the wine. Batya said *Hamotzi* (the blessing
over bread), and the bread was dipped in maple syrup

rather than salt since they were still in the first year of their marriage.

The Shabbat Meal

All ten people sat at a dining table that filled up the entire living space, so that we were all backed up against furniture, and no one (except Keturah and Levanah) got up throughout the meal. Here is the menu: Turkey neck soup. Roast chicken. Kugel. Beets. Salad. Challah. Fantastic chocolate cake—Batya found the recipe on the *Gourmet Magazine* page of the World Wide Web. Wine. Absolut. Southern Comfort. (The "hard" liquor appeared halfway through dinner.) Everyone drank, small amounts, toasting a good story:

"Reb Shlomo used to say . . . "

"No, that was the story that Reb Zalman said that Reb Shlomo said that the Izbitzer Rebbe said . . . "

"L'Chaim, L'Chaim . . . "

When the dessert was over, people said, "Could you hand over that text by So-and-so . . ." and "Do you happen to have . . . ", and Batya, nearest to the bookshelves, handed over texts and said, "These are the after-dinner mints," and everyone laughed and agreed.

Yossi got so involved in translating some lines of a particular text that he was intent upon sharing that Keturah and Levanah did some serious falling down without him noticing it, and Batya finally suggested to them that they "stop jumping around for a little while."

Menachem asked Yael something about the role of *metta* (lovingkindness) practice in Tibetan teachings, and she said something about it as one of the Six Perfections, and we spoke a bit about *metta* as an attribute of clear mind as contrasted with *metta* as a practice. Moshe was warming up to reading a certain text he had located, but by that time Keturah and Levanah seemed tired. Menachem said, "Moshe, why don't you lead the *bentsh*ing (blessing after meals)?" We all blessed, and then everyone walked home in the heavy rain. It was after eleven. We had started, with *Kiddush* (Sabbath wine blessing), at seven.

Lineage

I HAVE JEWISH LINEAGE. IT BEGAN WITH MY BIRTH IN a Jewish household that nourished it with stories and song and prayer and tradition that seem to have written themselves into my neuronal fibers. They are the language of my heart. I am thrilled to be able to tell my grandchildren stories I heard as a child. And I expect they will pass on to *their* grandchildren the stories I tell them about my grandparents.

One story I love to tell about my grandfather shows *his* steadfast lineage loyalty. My grandfather had no formal education in Europe. He could read prayer-book Hebrew, because his father had taught it to him. He gave up his daily prayer practice when he arrived in America at age twenty-five. Forty years later, after his wife died, he came to live in my household. The local East Third Street Shul got wind of his presence. I started to be awakened regularly by the phone very early in the morning.

"Ring!!" I'd reach out and grope for the extension next to my bed.

"Fischel," a voice would say in Yiddish, "We need a tenth for a *minyan!*" A few minutes later the back door would slam shut as my grandfather left for *shul*.

I also have a lineage affiliation to the Buddha. I am still, after ten years of teaching, awed each time I begin a Dharma talk, a presentation of Buddhist understanding. I feel I am taking my place in a lineage of teachers who have given variations of this same talk for more than two thousand years.

Near the end of his life the Buddha gave a discourse to a group of monks he was sending out to teach all over India. "Go forth, O monks," he said, "and teach the Dharma in the idiom of the people." My guess is that he meant, "You don't need to speak in Pali. You should teach in the local dialect so people will understand." I think of my principal teachers who are Americans and contemporaries, and appreciate how easily I learned from them because they shared my culture and my language. When I teach, I speak in the idiom of a sixty-year-old American-born woman with children and grandchildren, and I tell householder stories. When I teach in exclusively Jewish settings, I also feel free to include Psalm references and prayer references. They are also my idiom.

When I teach mindfulness, I mention that the Buddha listed four postures for practice: sitting, standing up, lying down, and walking. I remind Jews that the V'ahavta prayer mandates loving God "sitting in your house, walking on the road, lying down, and standing up." I take seriously the Buddha's injunction that teachings be explained so that they can be understood, and so I think he would be pleased with my teaching. I imagine the Buddha's voice, through two millenia of transmissions, telling me, "Go forth . . . "

I enjoy telling students about this teaching of the Buddha and reminding them that all of us—Dharma teachers and dentists and dancers and manicurists and mothers and monks—are transmitters of the truths we know through our relationships and that we are, all of us, sacred lineage holders. Often I end retreats by saying, "Go forth, O friends. . . . "

This Is How American Buddhism Looks

CATHY, A MEMBER OF THE SPIRIT ROCK COMMUNITY,
saw me sitting at a sidewalk cafe in Sonoma and sat down
to talk. "I went to James's class in Berkeley last night," she
said. "It was great. I cried. James always speaks so directly
from his heart. I've come to expect that from him. When I
go to Jack's class, I know it will be poetic. Afterwards, I'm
not always entirely sure what he talked about, but I always
feel moved. And Guy is so clear, so methodical, so orderly.
It's funny, seeing how everyone is so different. Everyone is
saying the same thing, but it sounds different."

"I think that's because wisdom is invisible," I said,
laughing because her characterizations of my friends were
so straightforward. "It doesn't change people's style. We
are all getting kinder and happier, I think, but we're all
still just us."

"Do you want to know your style?" Cathy asked.

"Sure I do," I said, wondering if I *really* did, but not willing to miss a good story.

"I tell my friends," Cathy said, "I go to Sylvia's class because she's so matter-of-fact, so practical. Also, you're
funny."

"Whew!" I thought, relieved. And I said, "I think a wonderful thing about Buddhism in America is that it's going
to roll through us, and we'll all be just who we always were,
only better."

Even before my book *It's Easier Than You Think* was in
the stores, an excerpt from it was published in the
Shambhala Sun, a newspaper of the American Tibetan

Buddhist community. I brought a copy to my Wednesday Spirit Rock class. Some of the people there have been my Dharma friends for years and knew many of the stories in the book. They were excited for me.

Someone said, "Why don't you read to us? See how it is to read out loud."

"Okay," I said, opening to the page, putting on my glasses. "I'm excited to be doing this."

"Is this *really* the first time you're reading the book in public?"

Without looking up I recognized the voice of Florence, one of a group of Jewish women from Berkeley who come regularly to class. I think Florence was reminding me of the "first-time" blessing.

I said, "Yes, it really is. And so, 'I bless the Source of creation that has kept me alive and sustained me and enabled me to reach this time.'" And then I read. Everyone applauded the story. The people for whom the blessing was meaningful were pleased. The people to whom it was not familiar probably didn't notice. Nobody minds, everyone listens, everyone applauds.

I remember seeing someone I admired—I think it was Gloria Steinem—interviewed on television on her fortieth birthday. The talk show host, probably as a compliment, said, "You don't look forty!"

"Yes, I do," she replied. "This is how forty looks."

I think the same answer works for Buddhism in America as well. It looks like modern America. Women and men. Old and young. Some monastics. Mostly lay people. Some people interested in incorporating Buddhist ritual practice into their lives. Some people (most, I think) interested in studying what the Buddha taught, dedicated to practicing clarity and lovingkindness. Some people are not connected to another religious tradition. Some, like myself, are connected. This is how American Buddhism looks.

Last Page

IT WOULD BE EASY TO READ MY STORY AND THINK, "Well, that happened to Sylvia because she grew up in a traditional and comfortable Jewish home." In fact, when I talk to other Jews who are Buddhists and who feel reinspired in their Judaism, their backgrounds are often quite different from mine. Some had painful family experiences. Others had painful Jewish experiences. Some people had minimal Jewish experiences. And not every single Jew who does Buddhist practice becomes reinspired. So if there is a particular formula for reinspiring one to Judaism, I don't know it.

Even as I think of my own story and my own reawakening, I can only speculate. It might be because I had mysterious experiences while I was meditating; it might also be because my background in Judaism was an affectionate and nurturing one; it might be because I have enough background in Judaism, one that I am currently, happily augmenting, so that Jewish texts and Jewish prayer and Jewish liturgy interest me and delight me.

It might also be that at crucial times in my life, times when I felt especially loved, it was in the context of Judaism. My grandmother and Mrs. Levy, in the context of the East Third Street Shul, made me feel loved. I fell in love with Zalman when I heard him *davven* with the Aquarian Minyan, because I got excited about the idea that it was possible to feel, as an adult, unembarrassed about trying to love God. Miles said, "I love you, and I think it would be a good idea for you to have a prayer practice." Rabbi

Sheinberger, in Jerusalem, was not frightened by my Buddhism and said, "I think you should read Moshe Chaim Luzatto," which was another way, I think, of saying "I love you." Most of all, my parents, who were cheerful, kind, best friends, loved me enormously, and they were Jews.

Acknowledgments

My friend Stephen Mitchell held the vision of this book for me since its beginning. His generous counsel, his insistence ("You can be more clear. Sit with this. Write it again. Let's talk"), and his confidence ("You can *so* do it") have sustained and inspired me.

I cannot imagine writing this book had my friend Rabbi Miles Krassen not said, "You are an even better teacher when you let your *yiddishkeit* show" and "I think you need a prayer practice. I'll teach you."

Rabbi Sheila Weinberg and I met at a Jewish-Buddhist conference and our personal dialogue and close friendship have grown since that time. Sheila read this book as I wrote it, correcting and encouraging, and I am grateful to her.

My friendship with Rabbi Helen Cohn includes breakfasts and lunches at which we share our spiritual questions and the insights of our prayer lives. Helen read the almost-final manuscript and offered valuable suggestions.

Jack Kornfield, my first Buddhist teacher, now my teaching colleague and my friend, read the manuscript during a camping trip with his family in Yosemite. He located a phone booth to call me with praise and suggestions.

Sharon Salzberg, my *metta* teacher, my teaching colleague, and my friend, also read the final manuscript and called with last-minute critical clarifications.

John Loudon, my editor at Harper San Francisco, showed admirable skill and unflagging courtesy as he shepherded this book through its unanticipated complex development.

As always, working with my friend and editorial assistant Martha Ley was a joy.

Thank-you, all.